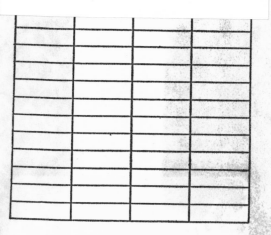

Images of disability on television

JOSEPH SHUMAN
JOURNALISM COLLECTION

POINT PARK COLLEGE

Images of disability on television

Guy Cumberbatch and Ralph Negrine
Broadcasting Research Unit

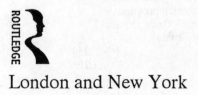

London and New York

First published 1992
by Routledge
11 New Fetter Lane, London EC4P 4EE

Simultaneously published in the USA and Canada
by Routledge
a division of Routledge, Chapman and Hall, Inc.
29 West 35th Street, New York, NY 10001

© 1992   Broadcasting Research Unit

Typeset by NWL Editorial Services, Langport, Somerset

Printed and bound in Great Britain
by Biddles Ltd, Guildford and King's Lynn

British Library Cataloguing in Publication Data
Images of disability on television.
   1. Great Britain. Handicapped persons. Related to
television.   2. United States. Handicapped persons. Related
to television.
I. Broadcasting Research Unit
791.4563520816

Library of Congress Cataloging in Publication Data
Images of disability on television/Broadcasting Research Unit.
   p.   cm.
   Includes bibliographical references (p.   ) and index.
   1. Handicapped in television. 2. Television programs –
United States. 3. Television programs – Great Britain. I.
Broadcasting Research Unit (Great Britain)
PN1992.8.H36I48   1991   91–11154
305.9′0816 – dc20   CIP

ISBN 0–415–06345–0

Contents

Tables

Acknowledgements

The Broadcasting Research Unit is greatly indebted to three groups for making this study possible and bringing it to completion.

First, we are deeply grateful to the funders of the research: to the BBC, the IBA, the ITV Fund and Channel 4. All four generously and unhesitatingly provided a quarter of the funds required for what was clearly seen by each of them as an important piece of work.

Second, we acknowledge with warm appreciation the skills and dedication of those who worked over an extended period of time on the various aspects of the research. The work was in effect divided into two, and the division is reflected in the two parts of the report. One part – a detailed content analysis of six weeks of television programming in 1988 – was carried out, under the leadership of Dr Guy Cumberbatch, by himself and his co-workers at Aston University: Matthew Lee, Dr Brown, Tim Watson, Yvonne Grice, Jacqui Woon and Rob Tinsley. The other part of the project – involving interviews and group discussions and a public opinion survey – was initiated by the late Sophie O'Neill, who provided a particularly eloquent and moving account of her interviews, and then completed by Dr Ralph Negrine of the University of Leicester. He was given active and willing assistance by Robin McGregor, Director of Special Projects in the BBC Broadcasting Research Department, and by Seona Reid.

Third, we are deeply grateful to the people with disabilities who first suggested the research subject to us and gave the initial impetus for its being undertaken. We trust that they will take not only interest but some satisfaction from the results of their initiative.

Finally, the BRU must thank its own: Dr David Morrison, who developed and set up the research, and Dr Michael Tracey, who committed the Unit to this important piece of work, before they

moved on to other challenges elsewhere; and Alison Joseph, who so
ably put the finishing touches to the report and steered it through to
publication.

As the editor of the report and Director of the BRU, I am pleased
to record my very grateful thanks to all those named and unnamed
who contributed to this research and this volume.

Tim Leggatt
December 1990

Introduction

This report, on the portrayal of people with disabilities on British television, is based upon research carried out in 1988 and the beginning of 1989. The first enquiry was designed to examine the actual portrayal on television of people with disabilities: both the extent of that portrayal and the manner of it. The object was to assess how adequately people with disabilities were being portrayed, both quantitatively – that is, how often and how many – and qualitatively – that is, in what manner and with what understanding and intention. The second enquiry was designed to assess reaction to this portrayal and to provide a commentary upon it.

The first part of the report is based on a content analysis of television programmes put out in peak viewing time, to viewers in the Birmingham area, during six weeks in the summer and autumn of 1988. All appearances of people with disabilities were counted and classified; and the tallies were then compared with what is known about the actual incidence of people with disabilities in the UK population, based upon the recent survey carried out by the Office of Population Censuses and Surveys (OPCS – published in 1988).

It might seem that this comparison between people or characters with disabilities and the objective assessment of the UK population by a Government office is uncontentious, but this is not so. It raises sharply the question of definition. We felt obliged to follow the OPCS definitions in order to be in a position to make comparisons between the population observed and the actual population of the country. However, the definitions used by the OPCS are strongly contended and questioned, especially by people with disabilities themselves. To put the matter briefly, many people with disabilities believe that it is not appropriate for them to be defined as such by able-bodied people, because then part of the experience of 'disability' that such people experience is a consequence of being so defined. There is therefore dispute as to whether the appropriate definition to use is one which is medically based or one which is based on social definition. In the report that follows much attention is given to this dispute and the difficulties which it raises.

Part I of the report is not only concerned with counting; it is also greatly concerned with the nature of the portrayal of people with disabilities, since one of the impulses behind the whole study was the belief that such people were not only underrepresented but also portrayed in a way that might be described as either manipulative or condescending. The content analysis therefore explored such questions, and also compared the portrayal of people with disabilities in UK and imported US drama productions, including films.

Part II of this report is based on discussion: on discussion groups held with people who themselves had disabilities, with those who care professionally for people with disabilities and with those from families in which someone has a disability. Also included were discussions with able-bodied people with no such experience. This commentary is also based upon interviews and discussions with writers and producers of programmes in which characters with disabilities are portrayed, in order to explore their attitudes and the constraints within which they work.

Finally, one chapter in Part II is based upon a survey of public attitudes towards certain issues concerned with people with disabilities. This was made possible through the help and co-operation of the BBC Research Department. It was not a large-scale survey and could deal with only a limited range of questions, but it does provide a means of linking the concerns of this enquiry to the attitudes and opinions of unselected television viewers.

The conclusion of the report is that the portrayal of people with disabilities on British television is indeed inadequate and that those who work in television should as a consequence give more thought to the portrayal of such people. A positive effort should now be made to deal with the issues raised by the inadequate and unsatisfactory representation of a substantial section of the population.

Part I

The portrayal of people with disabilities on television: a content analysis

Part I

The portrayal of people
with disabilities on
television: a content
analysis

Chapter 1

Introduction
Definitions and methods

DEFINING DISABILITY AND ISSUES OF TERMINOLOGY

The definition of disability is controversial. However, there are two sources of definitions which have helped to inform this study, those of the World Health Organisation (WHO) and the Department of Social Security (see Martin, Meltzer and Eliot, 1988). The WHO's International Classification of Impairment, Disability and Handicap provides a useful guide to different aspects of the definitional problem. They take impairment to be 'any loss or abnormality of psychological, physiological or anatomical structure or function' (WHO, 1980, p. 27). Disability is then taken as 'any restriction or lack (resulting from an impairment) of ability to perform an activity in the manner or within the range considered normal for a human being' (p. 28). Handicap is defined as 'a disadvantage for a given individual, resulting from an impairment or disability, that limits or prevents the fulfilment of a role (depending on age, sex and social and cultural factors) for that individual' (WHO, 1980, p. 29). The implication of these definitions is that impairment is a personal characteristic which can lead to the more social conditions of disability and handicap via the constraints imposed by the human environment. For example, skeletal impairment leads to difficulty or disability in walking and, in a hostile or unsupportive environment, to a mobility handicap. But the definition of impairment itself is inevitably informed by normative beliefs about what it is proper for people's bodies and minds to be like, and so we must concede a thoroughgoing normative element in all these definitions. This is not to deny that great pain and hardship may result from many conditions of impairment, but to insist that, particularly with the categories of disability and handicap,

the social environment influences who is included in the categories
and what their lives are like as a result.

The other readily available definition is the social security
definition where loss of faculty is defined as 'any pathological
condition (or any loss including a reduction) of the normal physical
or mental function of some organ or part of the body ... including
disfigurement' (quoted in Martin *et al.*, p. 8). Disability is defined as
the loss of a faculty which results in an inability to do things or do
them as well as a person of the same age and sex whose physical and
mental condition is normal. Disablement is the overall effect of the
relevant disabilities, that is, the overall inability to perform the
normal activities of life, the loss of health, strength and power to
enjoy a normal existence. Again it is clear that a strong normative
component is involved in the definition.

The Office of Population Censuses and Surveys (OPCS) (Martin
et al., 1988) operates with a slightly different concept of disability.
The overall rationale of its 1988 enquiry was stated thus:

> It was decided that the study would identify people with
> disabilities by asking directly about disabilities and would not
> cover impairments (except when thought necessary to ensure that
> people with disabilities such as those caused by mental or
> physiological problems were not missed).
>
> (p. 8)

What we shall mean in this study by disability is different from all of
these approaches and will be discussed in the following section,
where the coding schedule for the content analysis is described. In
examining the portrayal of disabled people on television we are
interested in the physical limitations that they exhibit and the social
milieux that they are depicted in.

For the moment let us state that we recognise the difficulty of
using a concept like disability, which implies that the deficiency or
impairment lies in the individual affected. We are aware of the
political nature of this implication, and the argument that the
handicaps, the disabilities and perhaps even the impairments are
apparent only because the environment is designed by and for the
able-bodied (see Chapter 7). Moreover, the umbrella term 'the
disabled' masks enormous diversity and obscures the individual
dignity of those who are included in the category. What disability
means to broadcasters, disability activists and disabled people in

broadcasting is described in O'Neill (1988) and also in Chapter 7. From this it is clear that even the liberal exhortation to consider people with disabilities as people first and disabled second does not satisfy some more politicised disability activists who assert that disability is a political category. This may perhaps remind able-bodied society of its responsibility for making a world where some people's characteristics make them unable to function effectively and its consequent responsibility for relieving this inbuilt discrimination. In this report we will use the terms 'people with disabilities' and 'disabled people' interchangeably, while recognising their shortcomings.

THE SAMPLE AND THE CODING SCHEDULE

This part of the study was devised to provide a detailed account of disability as observed on peak time television. Six weeks were selected in 1988 in which the peak viewing time programmes of all four channels transmitted in the Birmingham area were recorded. These were the four weeks from 9th May 1988 to 5th June 1988, the week from the 24th to the 30th of October, and the week from the 14th to the 20th of November 1988. On sampling days recording generally began around 6 p.m. but was varied slightly so that the sample included only whole programmes. On BBC1 weekday recording generally began with the popular soap *Neighbours* at 5.30 p.m., on ITV (Central Television) with the *News at 5.45* and on BBC2 and Channel 4 at the programme break nearest to this time. Recording finished usually around 11 p.m., again at a convenient programme break. We shall call this sample of programmes the main or official sample, which is representative of peak viewing output. In addition, a supplementary or boost sample of 148 programmes (mainly films) which were judged to be of interest to this project were recorded and analysed, even though they fell outside the official sampling period. It should be noted that whereas this boost sample would give a misleading impression of the frequencies with which people with disabilities appeared on television, it broadens the basis from which to analyse the way in which they were portrayed. Thus, in discussing the representation of disabled people in dramatic fiction, our estimates of their prevalence will be based on the official sample but our account of how they were portrayed will be based on both the official and boost samples.

The objectives of our coding schedule were twofold. First, it aimed to record the number of characters appearing on peak time television and to allow us to calculate the percentage of the population of characters who were disabled. Secondly, we were interested in the types of roles characters play, to allow the able-bodied to be compared to people with disabilities. Two schedules were used to code the characters appearing on television: a general schedule which was intended to capture the nature of the characters and their life, and a medical list, as used by the OPCS in their study of disability in the UK population. The purpose of this was to enable some comparisons to be made between the population on television and the actual population of the UK. A full account of the characteristics of disabled characters which were coded in our study can be found in the coding schedule and the copy of the OPCS medical list supplied in the appendices. We distinguish between four kinds of character roles in fiction programmes, namely (i) major characters, who were central to the plot, with high visibility and large speaking roles, (ii) minor characters, who were not central to the plot, with small speaking roles or occasional appearances, (iii) incidental characters, who were not part of the plot but appeared with perhaps a few lines, and finally (iv) background characters, who served merely to fill in, for example, people in bars or in the background in outdoor scenes. The bulk of our detailed analysis of disability in fiction concentrates on major and minor characters.

We are concerned with a range of variables and issues surrounding disability. As well as information on the frequency with which various kinds of handicap appear, we are interested in the apparent state of mind of the disabled person, whether they seem content, whether they are preoccupied with their problems and whether disability is regularly associated with criminality or psychopathology. We attempted to code a set of personal variables for each disabled person who appeared. These ranged from independence and extroversion, to whether the person seemed to be liked and was socially accepted, to whether they were married or had access to sexual experience. We were interested too in the social setting, in whether their freedom was curtailed and whether they were presented in a context of achievement or despondency and whether the able-bodied appear to disempower or infantilise disabled people. In order to capture some sense of the evolving storyline some of these variables were coded for the first, middle and final thirds of the programme. Disabled characters were compared with a sample of selected 'normal' able-bodied characters from the same television programmes to investigate any differences in presentation.

Two points must be made about our concerns. First, they reflect the breadth of focus, from impairment to handicap, given in the WHO classification, and second, they are informed by current debates about the position of disabled people in society. An inspection of our coding schedule will reveal how exhaustive we managed to be, but our topics of interest are informed by the social context in which this study was carried out.

Chapter 2

Frequencies in the portrayal of disability on television

In this chapter we review the results of our analysis of the frequency with which people with disabilities appeared on television. First we will be concerned with the overall frequency pattern of disability on television; then we shall make some comparisons between US and UK television programmes, consider channel differences and provide an account of how we assessed the proportion of disabled characters in the television population. Finally, we will be concerned with the relationship between the rate, severity and kinds of disabilities depicted in fictional programmes and those found in the UK population.

TYPES OF PROGRAMME AND THE DEPICTION OF DISABILITY

During the six sampling weeks a total of 1,286 programmes were recorded and coded. In addition the supplementary sample of 148 programmes, mainly films, from outside the sampling period were included because we believed that these would be of particular interest to the study. We may roughly divide our sample into factual programmes – all those which purport to be a direct presentation of reality, such as news, current affairs, documentaries and magazine programmes – and entertainment or drama programmes which contain fictional characters. We shall call these 'factual' and 'fictional' programmes respectively, although these category titles are rough approximations to the relationship which a programme's producers might intend it to have to reality. Of our sample, 804 programmes were classified as factual and 482 as fictional. Thus nearly two-thirds (63 per cent) were factual programmes and just over one-third fictional (37 per cent). In total, 211 programmes of the

Table 2.1 Frequencies with which the main genres of factual programmes occurred and the numbers containing reference to or depiction of disability

Genre	No. of progs.	Percentage of total progs.	No. with disability	Percentage of total with disability
News	221	27	54	42
Current affairs	28	4	0	0
Documentary	155	19	21	16
Magazine	70	9	20	16
Informational	59	7	4	3
Debate	15	2	2	2
Religious	9	1	2	2
Quiz	24	3	3	2
Music/dance	38	5	0	0
Educational	5	0.6	2	2
Game show	44	5	0	0
Chat show	24	3	4	3
Sport	36	4	1	1
Special broadcast	46	6	12	9
Special interest programme	3	0.4	3	2
Other	27	3	0	0
Total	804	99	128	100

1,286 sampled included people with disabilities, that is, 16.4 per cent of all programmes. A further 23 programmes (1.8 per cent of all programmes) mentioned disability but did not show any disabled people. Table 2.1 gives the distribution of the different genres of factual programme and the number containing disability.

We may notice that 42 per cent of the factual programmes containing disability were news broadcasts, with documentary and magazine programmes accounting for another 32 per cent. In Chapter 3 we will be examining the treatment of people with disabilities in factual programmes in more depth, but first let us look at the distribution of programmes featuring disability among the fictional genres. Table 2.2 gives the main fictional genres and the numbers of these which featured disability.

Overall, 17 per cent of fictional programmes portrayed disability but the distribution of programmes with disability includes a

Table 2.2 Frequencies with which the main genres of fictional programmes occurred and the numbers containing reference to or depiction of disability

Genre	No. of progs.	Percentage of total progs.	No. with disability	Percentage of total with disability
Crime/police/ detective	37	8	12	15
Thriller	15	3	4	5
Spy	2	0.4	1	1
Western	6	1	2	2.5
War	8	2	3	4
Historical drama	11	2	5	6
Other drama	104	21	26	32.5
Science fiction	3	1	0	0
Horror	1	0.2	1	1
Soap	98	20	8	10
Avant-garde	1	0.2	0	0
Comedy	24	5	2	2.5
Sitcom	93	19.3	8	10
Light entertainment	25	5	3	4
Cartoon	13	3	0	0
Children's drama	17	3.5	4	5
Other children's prog.	15	3	0	0
Opera	1	0.2	0	0
Play	6	1	1	1
Fantasy	2	0.4	0	0
Total	482	99.2	80	99.5

relatively large number of 'other drama programmes', that is, drama programmes which do not easily fit into any of the other categories. Of the more precisely defined genres, crime, police and detective programmes are noteworthy, as they provide 15 per cent of fictional programmes which include people with disabilities, while soaps and sitcoms provide 10 per cent each.

The type of programme most likely to include people with disabilities was feature films, of which 41 per cent portrayed characters with disabilities. If we divide up the programming in a slightly different way, we can bring out the relationship between films and other kinds of programme. Of the 549 factual programmes coded, 128 (23 per cent) portrayed disabled people. Nearly half (46 per cent) of this 23 per cent were news programmes. Thus overall nearly a quarter (24 per cent) of news broadcasts showed disability.

COMPARING UK AND US FICTIONAL PROGRAMMES

American programmes play an important role in British television schedules. During our sample period 11 per cent of the programmes coded were US produced, the vast majority of which fell into the drama categories. If we look at drama programmes alone (of which we coded 404) we find that 60 per cent of them were UK produced while 31 per cent originated in the US. The UK was responsible for 242 drama programmes, of which 15 per cent contained a portrayal of a disabled character. Of the 124 US productions 27 per cent contained such a portrayal. However, this figure indicates only the frequencies, and we will deal with genre differences between the two countries and the types of roles played by disabled characters in a later section. For the moment let us remind ourselves that this does not necessarily mean that a higher proportion of US programmes as a whole contain disability, since we are dealing only with a sample which has been bought and selected for broadcast in the UK and is probably not representative of US programming.

CHANNEL DIFFERENCES

Let us now consider differences between channels in terms of their inclusion of disabled people. By channel, the proportion of programmes that contained people with disabilities was the same for ITV and BBC1, both channels portraying disabled people in 20 per cent of programmes. The proportions were also similar for Channel 4 and BBC2, both of which portrayed people with disabilities in 12 per cent of programmes. The greatest channel differences were found in factual programmes, the percentage featuring disabled characters being comparable in the channels' fiction output. Table 2.3 gives the numbers of programmes and the percentages falling into each category.

The differences between the channels in respect of the number of programmes portraying disabled people were concentrated in news coverage and seem to be mainly due to the lack of regional news on Channel 4. News programmes had a relatively high incidence of people with disabilities, who appeared in 24 per cent of all news

Table 2.3 Number of programmes containing reference to or depiction of disability, by channel

Production type	BBC1 A	B	C	BBC2 A	B	C	ITV A	B	C	C4 A	B	C
Factual	226	53	23%	163	17	10%	193	42	22%	212	16	8%
Fiction	159	24	15%	88	14	16%	136	24	18%	109	21	19%
Total	385	77	20%	251	31	12%	329	66	20%	321	37	12%

Key
A = Total number of programmes of each production type
B = Total number of production type containing reference to or depiction of disability
C = Percentage of production type containing reference to or depiction of disability

programmes. Only 7 per cent of the total number of news programmes in our sample originated from BBC2, thus contributing to the low incidence of disabled people coded on this channel. Channel 4 provided 17 per cent of the news programmes but only 13 per cent of these contained disabled people. As we have suggested, this is mainly due to the fact that Channel 4 does not broadcast any regional news, and regional news accounted for 38 per cent of all news programmes that contained people with disabilities. Additionally, as Channel 4 provided only one news programme per night in our peak viewing time sampling period, it did not repeat any stories, and there were no 'human interest' types of stories such as charity events or awards ceremonies involving people with disabilities. These types of stories accounted for 28 per cent of the stories involving people with disabilities on BBC1 and ITV's news bulletins. Channel differences were also noted in current affairs and documentary programmes. On BBC 1 these made up 9 per cent of the total number of factual programmes, and 24 per cent of them contained disabled people. On ITV they made up 16 per cent, and 19 per cent of these contained disabled people; on BBC 2 they made up 38 per cent of factual programmes with 12 per cent containing disabled people, and on Channel 4 they made up 33 per cent of factual programmes with 3 per cent containing disabled people.

ESTIMATING THE RATE OF DISABILITY IN TELEVISION DRAMA

So far, we have been concerned with the overall numbers of programmes which contained disabled people or discussed disability. A further part of our analysis concerned the characters who were presented in television drama. As part of the coding of dramatic fiction programmes, a count was made of the number of characters appearing in these productions. Dramatic fiction was operationally defined as any programme featuring fictional characters. This included films, drama series, soap operas and situation comedies. It did not include fictional characters where they intruded into factual programmes. If Sherlock Holmes is discussed in factual programmes, this does not turn them into dramatic fiction. The total number of characters that appeared during the six week sampling period was 35,798, of whom 2,469 were considered to be major characters who were central to the plot, 2,298 were minor characters with speaking roles (assuming they did not have a disability which prevented speech), 2,144 were incidental characters appearing briefly, usually with one or two lines, and 28,887 were background characters.

From the total number of major and minor characters a subsample was drawn for further analysis. We selected the first able-bodied major or minor character to appear after the programme had been running for 10 minutes, a second character was selected in the same way from mid-way through the programme, and a third character was drawn 10 minutes further into the programme. In addition, all the major or minor characters with disabilities were included. This resulted in a sample of 1,689 characters selected for more detailed coding.

It is instructive to examine the demographic make-up of this subsample, which is likely to be representative of people appearing in television drama as a whole. Analysis of this subsample suggests that 95 per cent of the television population were white, 65 per cent were male, over 50 per cent were between the ages of 25 and 40, 19 per cent were professionals or white-collar workers and 6 per cent were unemployed. Of the 4,767 major and minor characters appearing in dramatic fiction, 66 had some sort of disability, thus suggesting that 1.4 per cent of the major and minor characters in television drama had disabilities. (See Chapter 4 for further discussion of this.)

The figures for incidental and background characters were even lower, with 24 incidental and 92 background characters coded, giving rates of disability of 1.1 per cent and 0.3 per cent respectively. This is particularly low when it is considered that, according to the Office of Population, Censuses and Surveys (Martin, Meltzer and Eliot, 1988), 14 per cent of the UK population have some kind of disability. Before we condemn broadcasters outright, however, we should attempt to place this in context, for example, by allowing for the different age profiles of the populations on television and in the UK. In the following section we will discuss further the issues that arise in making comparisons between television and real world populations.

RATES OF DISABILITY IN DRAMATIC FICTION COMPARED WITH RATES IN THE UK POPULATION

In this section we will consider the relationship between the rates of disability in the population as a whole given by the OPCS survey (Martin *et al.*, 1988) and those shown on television in dramatic fiction. Research into television content has regularly been concerned with comparisons between content data and data pertaining to the wider society. Early work by Smythe (1954) and Head (1954) compared the demographic profiles of characters on TV with those in the population, using census data. More recent accounts can be found in Greenberg *et al.*'s Life on Television (1980) and in Signorelli (1984). Most of this work is based on US TV and society and there is a relative lack of work on British TV and on disability. The central conceptual strand of this type of work is captured by von Feilitzen *et al.* (1989) who say that

> the TV content (or usually some part of it) is thought of as a symbolic world, often called the TV world, and this world is compared with that existing outside television.
>
> (p. 11)

Moreover

> we intend to show that the TV world may be conceived of in several ways, each generating particular methodological demands and operational definitions. We further show that these distinctions tend to produce different empirical results.
>
> (p. 12)

In this section we will consider different ways of estimating the prevalence of disabled people on television from our data, and how to compare these with the UK population.

As we have already mentioned, the rate of disability among major and minor characters in dramatic fiction was found to be 1.4 per cent, which apparently contrasts unfavourably with the figure of 14 per cent in the population given by the OPCS survey. But the incidence of disability in the population as a whole is related to age, such that 3.1 per cent of the population aged between 20 and 29 is disabled, a proportion which rises to 40.8 per cent of the population between 70 and 79 years old. Table 2.4 gives a comparison of age-related rates of disability between the television and UK populations.

As we can see, the television and UK populations have a very different age profile, with 20–50-year-olds being overrepresented and 60 + -year-olds being underrepresented in the television population. Given this age profile on television we can calculate an expected number of people with disabilities on television, as shown in Table 2.5.

From these figures the percentage of people with disabilities which we would expect to see on television is $(108/1,587) \times 100 = 6.81$

Table 2.4 Age comparison of UK population and television population

Age group	UK population Number	Percentage	Cumulative percentage	Television population Number	Percentage	Cumulative percentage
70+	5 891 107	13.5	13.5	17	1.1	1.1
60–69	5 558 333	12.7	26.2	79	5.0	6.1
50–59	5 962 406	13.6	39.8	154	9.7	15.8
40–49	6 471 429	14.8	54.6	342	21.6	37.4
30–39	7 772 727	17.8	72.4	527	33.2	70.6
20–29	8 516 129	19.5	91.9	395	24.9	95.5
16–19	3 619 050	8.3	100.2	73	4.6	100.1
Total	43 791 181			1587		

Note: Figures for under 16-year-olds were not included in the OPCS report but in the television population there were 83, bringing the total to 1670

Table 2.5 Expected number of people with disabilities in the television population

Age range	Number of people in TV population	Percentage of people expected to be disabled (OPCS)	Expected number of disabled people in TV population
70+	17	40.8	7
60–69	79	24.0	19
50–59	154	13.3	21
40–49	342	7.0	24
30–39	527	4.4	23
20–29	395	3.1	12
16–19	73	2.1	2
Total	1587		108

Table 2.6 Percentage of disabled characters appearing in dramatic fiction

Character role	Total number of characters	Number of disabled characters	Disabled characters as percentage of total characters
Major	2469	38	1.5
Minor	2298	28	1.2
Incidental	2144	24	1.1
Background	28887	92	0.3
Major and minor	4767	66	1.4
Total	35798	182	0.5

per cent. Using this figure the expected number of major and minor characters with a disability would be 6.81 per cent of the total of 4,767 who appeared during the six week sampling period, that is, 325 characters. In fact 66 major and minor characters with disabilities occurred in this period, one-fifth of the number that we would expect if the television population were to mirror the real world in this respect. Using the same expected percentage for incidental and background characters, the expected numbers would be 146 incidental and 1,967 background characters with disabilities which compares with the 24 incidental and 92 background characters actually coded. Table 2.6 gives further details.

In addition to the 66 major and minor disabled character appearances that were coded during the main sampling period, a further 88 were coded from the supplementary sample of 148 programmes. Comparing the depiction of disability in the two sets of programmes reveals that though there were relatively more disabled characters in the supplementary sample there was little difference between the make-up of the two groups. Of the total 154 major and minor disabled character appearances coded, the majority had a physical disability.

We will discuss the relationship between the profiles of disability apparent in the television population and the UK population in more detail below when we begin to fill in the picture concerning the kinds of disability which were featured. There are two ways of doing this, suggested by the OPCS survey, so we will deal first with the profile of severity of disabilities on television and then later with the profile of different kinds of disability portrayed on television.

COMPARING THE SEVERITY PROFILE OF DISABILITY ON
TELEVISION WITH THE SEVERITY PROFILE OF THE UK
POPULATION

Here we will examine the severity of the types of disabilities shown in
dramatic fiction. For this we will be using both the official six week
sample and the supplementary sample of 148 programmes. From
these sources we have altogether 118 programmes in which one or
more than one major or minor disabled character was coded, yielding
154 character appearances in total. It is worth remembering that our
figure of 154 does not represent 154 different people, since some
characters recurred in different episodes of the same series, for
example, Philip Marlow, played by Michael Gambon in Dennis
Potter's series *The Singing Detective*. Our figure of 154 represents 140
different characters. Unfortunately we do not have figures for the rate
of repetition of able-bodied characters in these programmes, and we
shall assume that they repeated at the same rate as disabled characters.

Our 154 character appearances include 66 which occurred in the
official sampling period, which corresponded to 2,469 major and
2,298 minor able-bodied character appearances. This gives a rate of
character appearance of 1.4 per cent. The remaining 88 character
appearances occurred in programmes which we selected because they
were likely to be of interest to the project, and are not likely to be
representative of television output as a whole. The OPCS survey
(Martin *et al.*, 1988) suggests that 14.2 per cent of the UK population
are disabled according to its definition, but given the age profile of
the television population we would expect (as demonstrated above)
only 6.81 per cent of the television population to show some sort of
disability. This process of correcting for age assumes that the world
of television is roughly like our own and that if old people do not
appear it is because they are not shown, rather than because they do
not exist; and it introduces the difficult issue of the relation between
the populations of the real world and the world of television. For
example, the population on television is an amalgam of people from
Britain, America and to a lesser degree other countries, whereas the
OPCS survey relates to Britain alone. As we shall discuss in the
conclusion, such a process is based also on a normative belief that the
television population should reflect the population as a whole. The
age correcting process does not excuse the low 1.4 per cent rate of
appearance of disabled characters, but it does place it in the context
of a wider set of discriminations, and introduces arguments about the

low rate of representation of other groups, such as old people, ethnic minorities and women, on television.

So far we have given an overall account of the rates of disability portrayed in the fictional TV population. Let us now begin to develop a more differentiated picture of these disabled people. Whereas there is some dispute about whether it is meaningful or legitimate to place disabilities in a hierarchy (see O'Neill, 1988), the severity of the disabilities is one dimension on which it is particularly easy to compare the television and UK populations, since the OPCS survey includes a severity scale from 1 to 10 on which disabilities may be assessed.

Briefly, the OPCS scale includes assessments on 14 dimensions of possible disability: locomotion; reaching and stretching; dexterity; personal care; continence; seeing; hearing; communication; behaviour; intellectual functioning; consciousness; eating, drinking and digestion; disfigurement; and other problems. On 11 of these dimensions there is a graduated scale of problems with a severity score assigned to each. Thus, for locomotion, being unable to walk at all gives a severity score of 11.5, whereas being unable to walk 400 yards without stopping or severe discomfort gives a severity score of 0.5. A copy of the OPCS coding guide can be found in Appendix I. In converting the individual severity scores into a total measure, the OPCS team combined the scores according to the formula: total severity score = worst score + 0.4 (second worst) + 0.3 (third worst). This figure is then translated into a set of categories from 1 to 10, with 1 being the least and 10 being the most severe. Only multiple disabilities can achieve a severity category of more than 6.

We attempted to calculate on this basis severity scores and severity categories for all 154 disabled character appearances in dramatic fiction. Our 154 cases include 14 characters under 16, whom we ignored because the OPCS survey concerns over-16s only; thus we would expect disabled adults to appear in the TV population at an age-adjusted rate of 6.19 per cent. We added a category, called 0, to accommodate those cases which were not amenable to coding into OPCS categories or which did not receive a sufficiently high score to enter category 1. To calculate the rate of disability in the virtual population on television we took the 154 cases to represent a proportion of disabled people in the television population, to compare with the rate in the real population calculated by the OPCS. The distribution of severity categories is given in Table 2.7.

The rate per 1,000 in the television population was calculated

Table 2.7 Distribution of severity categories of disability among major and minor characters in dramatic fiction and in the television and UK populations

Severity Category	Least severe 0	1	2	3	4	5	6	7	8	9	Most severe 10	Total
Frequency of characters	20	36	10	7	7	11	43	9	9	2	0	154
Under 16	3	2	0	0	1	1	4	0	3	0	0	14
Adults	17	34	10	7	6	10	39	9	6	2	0	140
Rate per 1000 TV population	7.5	15	4.4	3.1	2.7	4.4	17.2	4	2.7	0.9	0	61.9
Rate per 1000 real population (OPCS)	–	28	19	17	16	16	13	11	9	7	5	141

using the age-adjusted figure of 6.81 per cent as the numerator in the percentage term. This is not done because we are endorsing that figure or because we have forgotten the absolute figure of 1.4 per cent. We are using it because it illustrates the relative profiles of disability in the population and on television, since with this figure the two profiles intersect to indicate areas of under- and over-representation.

Of the 140 adults whom we attempted to code, 17 were not amenable to coding or were not disabled severely enough to be included in categories 1 to 10. Of the 123 cases left, the relatively less severe category 1 and the moderately severe 6 were most regularly achieved, with 34 and 39 entries respectively. Comparing the apparent rates in the TV population with the OPCS estimates for the real population we notice that the only category for which the TV rate exceeds the real rate is 6. Of the 39 character appearances which were coded into category 6, for 20 this was because they appeared to be unable to walk. Others appeared to be totally unable to see or hear. This might suggest something about the way in which television represents disability. Only 33 of the 140 adult character appearances exhibited sufficiently widespread disability to be coded under more than one of the terms on the OPCS list. Unless multiple disabilities are present, it is not possible for a person to achieve a score high enough to be placed in a category above 6. Television, then, seems to represent disability most regularly in terms of unidimensional problems. Moreover, there is some considerable reliance on the inability to walk or see or hear as a way of representing handicap.

THE PROFILE OF KINDS OF DISABILITY

Now let us look at the different kinds of disability exhibited in the television population. We have already performed an elementary classification of types of disability in terms of physical disability, mental illness, mental handicap and sensory disability, but now let us examine the profile of kinds of disability in terms of the OPCS grouping of disability types. In this, our method resembles that of Bourdieu (1984), who in his study of taste and value judgements classified his interview data in different ways in order to ensure that his overall results were not an artefact of a single classification procedure. As previously mentioned, the OPCS survey identifies 14 areas of disability. When comparing the various severity categories between the real and the television populations, we can calculate a

Table 2.8 Distribution of types of disability among major and minor characters in dramatic fiction and in the television and UK populations

OPCS disability group		Frequency of characters	Under 16	Adults	Rate per 1000 TV population	Rate per 1000 real population (OPCS)
0	Uncodable	12	2	10	42	–
I	Locomotion	54	7	47	196	99
II	Reaching/stretching	9	1	8	33	28
III	Dexterity	8	0	8	33	40
IV	Personal care	8	1	7	29	38
V	Continence	1	0	1	4	59
VI	Seeing	13	0	13	54	57
VII	Hearing	13	0	13	54	26
VIII	Communication	2	0	1	4	27
IX	Behaviour	27	0	27	112	31
X	Intellectual functioning	12	1	11	45	34
XI	Consciousness	1	1	0	0	5
XII	Eat, drink, digestion	3	1	2	8	6
XIII	Disfigurement	16	1	15	63	9*
XIV	Other	1	0	1	4	**

* 9 per thousand in private households, excluding institutions
** No OPCS figure given for this group

Note: Some character appearances contribute to more than one group

rough rate per thousand by making the assumption that the age corrected rate of disability in the television population, 6.8 per cent, can be used as the numerator in the percentage term. Thus we can achieve a rough comparison between the OPCS survey and the population that appears on television as in Table 2.8.

Again, it must be stressed that the rates per thousand calculated for the television population constitute a guide to the relative prevalence of disabilities falling into the different categories identified by the OPCS survey. However, some clear discrepancies between the rates for different groups in the population and on television deserve comment. Locomotor, behaviour and disfigurement problems are relatively overrepresented in the television population, whereas communication and continence problems are relatively underrepresented. We may explain the prevalence of locomotor, behaviour and disfigurement problems in terms of the visual nature of television: they are the easiest to represent, they are immediately apparent and can be used to connote a range of living difficulties which may accompany them. If we see someone in a wheelchair, then we may reflect on all the things that it is difficult to do, like catch buses, get in and out of bed, go to the toilet and so forth. Thus, a conspicuous locomotor difficulty allows for a very efficient representation, since it brings to mind a great deal in a single camera shot. Similarly, any form of mental incapacity, disorder or distress can be easily and efficiently represented by an outburst of temper, a suicide attempt, or unpleasantness to family and friends. Incontinence may be underrepresented because of lavatorial taboos, and communication problems are difficult to convey succinctly on television, perhaps because requiring extended sequences to establish the nature of the problem. Moreover, the representation of such disabilities may be less efficient at calling to mind the constellation of difficulties in living which they give rise to.

The nature of the locomotion problems might repay further study. The detective Ironside is confined to a wheelchair, and thus his mobility is restricted compared to his able-bodied colleagues; he is pushed about the room or wheels himself rather than walks, but this does not restrict his mobility around the city, nor does it prevent him getting to the upper floors of buildings. Ironside's restricted mobility is not allowed to restrict the plot or the settings of the programme.

A further set of reasons for the choice of disabilities featured on television can be suggested by reference to the ubiquity of the wheelchair as an index of disability, and the readiness with which it is called to mind in relation to disability. People working in television are both a part of our culture, and are themselves aware of it. Thus, when they want to include a disabled role, they are likely to think of locomotor handicaps necessitating a wheelchair, and that this is an icon of disability that the public will recognise.

CONSTRAINTS ON OUR INTERPRETATIONS

The comparisons between the UK population and the television population in this section must be thought of as a rough guide only. There are a number of reasons why this is so.

First, it must be remembered that the main unit of analysis has been the character appearance, not the individual character. Thus, in our sample, *The Singing Detective* occurred several times. For each programme the central character Philip Marlow would be recorded. Moreover, in each programme he would be coded differently, because during the series his psoriasis first became worse and then improved, so that he would be in different stages of disability. Herman Munster, on the other hand, is coded for each episode of *The Munsters*, but would be fairly constant in each. The OPCS team went to some trouble to ensure that no respondent was questioned twice. Our coding principle was adopted because we wanted our analysis to give a snapshot picture of disability on television. Our analysis would not have been made much more subtle by trying to trace individual characters from episode to episode, but it would have become much more time-consuming and expensive.

Second, the OPCS medical list in Martin et al. can be properly applied only via something similar to a clinical assessment interview, whereas television characters can be coded only in terms of what they do on screen. The specific problems listed in Martin *et al.* involve activities which are not regularly performed by characters on television so that characters' difficulties have to be translated into the terms of the medical list.

However, the relationship between profiles of disability in the television and real populations does tell us something about the dominant representational modes of television. The characters often either have problems which are relatively slight (in OPCS terms) or severe on one particular dimension. Also, there is considerable reliance on highly visual types of problem, like locomotion difficulties, behaviour problems and disfigurements.

Chapter 3

The portrayal of disability in factual programmes

In this chapter we will deal with the portrayal of disabled people in non-fiction or 'factual' programmes. Although there were more non-fictional than fictional programmes in the sample, the former will be dealt with rather more briefly than the latter in the chapters that follow. This is because the characteristics of non-fictional programmes can be summarised more succinctly and usually they do not have the richness of treatment, theme and storyline which a proper account of fictional genres necessitates.

Nearly two-thirds (63 per cent) of all 1,286 programmes coded during the six week sample period were factual ones (804). Nearly half of these (47 per cent) were either news (221) or documentary programmes (155). On average one in six (15.9 per cent) of all factual programmes contained someone who could be classified as 'disabled'. However, such appearances predominated in news programmes, which as a genre provided nearly a half (44 per cent) of all such cases.

As with fictional programmes, the disability most often presented was one of locomotor difficulty, which accounted for nearly one-third of all those people who could be classified as disabled.

Storylines

Before examining the manner in which people with disabilities were presented, the most obvious starting point for factual programmes is to categorise the storylines: what were the stories about? It seems clear that the diversity of stories is complicated by the centrality or otherwise of disability. However, some eleven categories provided a convenient classification of the story lines (see Table 3.3). This analysis included 19 programmes selected from outside the sampling

Table 3.1 Factual programmes containing reference to or depiction of disability, by genre

Genre	Number	Percentage	Proportion of progs in genre
News	54	42.2	24%
Documentary	21	16.4	13%
Magazine	20	15.6	29%
Special broadcast	12	9.4	26%
Informational	4	3.1	7%
Chat show	4	3.1	17%
Programme for disabled	3	2.3	All
Other	10	7.8	
Total	128	99.9	

period, bringing the total up to 147 factual programmes showing disability. Up to three storylines were coded for each programme.

The 'other' category in Table 3.3 was largely due to the presence of disabled people whose disabilities were incidental to the report. For example, on *News At Ten* (13/5/88) a report appeared about small pink frogs that fell from the sky onto an Oxfordshire village. For part of the time a partially deaf farmer was asked what he thought about the enthusiasm of the naturalists who had turned up to scour his pond in the hope of discovering some of the stray frogs. The farmer's disability was not an issue during the report, although the reasons for including the interview were perhaps questionable, since it seemed designed to emphasise the bizarre nature of the story.

NEWS PROGRAMMES

Overview of news and its storylines

Here, because of the importance of news as an informational genre, we will give special attention to the question of how news programmes portrayed disability. The depiction of disability on the news might give some clues about the role of disability in public life. News programmes made up over a quarter (27.3 per cent) of the factual programmes, and of the 221 news programmes broadcast during the 6 week sampling period 59 (26.7 per cent) contained a report or reports showing or discussing people with disabilities. Once

Table 3.2 Type of disability portrayed in factual programmes

Type of disability	Number	Percentage of total
Locomotion difficulties	74	31.6
Sensory disabilities: blind, partially sighted deaf, partially deaf	33	14.1
Physical disfigurement, including missing or malformed limbs and disfigurement of body or face	29	12.4
Invisible disabilities, including AIDS, heart disease and cancer	29	12.4
Cerebral palsy	18	7.7
Mental handicap	17	7.3
Brain damage	14	6.0
Mental illness	6	2.6
Other disabilities, including Down's Syndrome, disorientation and dyslexia	14	6.0
Total	234	100.1

again the types of stories in which people with disabilities appeared can be divided into 11 major categories. For this analysis 4 news programmes drawn from outside the sampling period, in which people with disabilities appeared, will be included.

A total of 63 news bulletins included people with disabilities: for each bulletin up to 3 of the above categories were coded; on average 3 storylines were identifiable in every 2 programmes.

Table 3.4 shows that the most prevalent types of stories associated with disabled people related to medical issues of some kind, namely treatments and cures, partial cures or potential cures for disabling illnesses. As with many news items, a number were part of a continuing story, and two stories made up over half (13) of the items

Table 3.3 Types of storyline in factual programmes including people with disabilities

	Number	Percentage of total
Treatment (medical)	37	16
Special achievement	26	11
Cure (examination of)	21	9
Normal achievement/fitting into normal life	20	9
Tragedy	17	7
Victim	16	7
Struggle for equality	15	7
Rehabilitation	15	7
Prejudice	8	3
Mixed	3	1
Other	52	23
Total	230	100

Table 3.4 Types of storyline in news bulletins including people with disabilities

	Number	Percentage of total
Treatment (medical)	21	22
Special achievement	11	11
Cure (examination of)	10	10
Victim	8	8
Tragedy	5	5
Struggle for equality	5	5
Normal achievement/fitting into normal life	4	4
Rehabilitation	3	3
Prejudice	3	3
Mixed	2	2
Other	25	26
Total	97	99

relating to the treatment of people with disabilities. The first was about the use of brain cells taken from foetuses and implanted into the brains of people with Parkinson's Disease. This story came up 7 times around the beginning of June 1988. Disability was essentially a side issue in the way in which the story was reported. Although the news angle was, initially at least, of a medical breakthrough, most attention was focused on the medical ethics of the procedure. The second most reported story had quite a different emphasis; it was

Table 3.5 Themes in news storylines

	Mentioned		Not mentioned		Total
Fitting into normal life	20	(32%)	43	(68%)	63
Lack of understanding by society or individuals	12	(19%)	51	(81%)	63
Physical progress of person with disability	19	(30%)	44	(70%)	63
Rights to fight for	11	(17%)	52	(83%)	63

about young children from Britain undergoing conductive education at the Peto Institute in Budapest. On all 6 occasions that this story was told there was factual commentary about the process of conductive education and how it helped children with cerebral palsy. Furthermore, the issue of under-funding for similar schools in Britain was raised on most occasions. However, in terms of stereo-typing there was a tendency to applaud the achievements and bravery of the children involved. An early report opened with the statement: 'Handicapped children are home from Hungary proud of their achievements' (ITV, 17/11/88), and this set the tone of the report as a success story.

Overall, nearly a quarter (23 per cent) of the 63 news stories relating to people with disabilities were to a large extent concerned with their achievements, as either out of the ordinary or managing to fit into a 'normal life'. Of the 15 reports that fell into this category, 4 involved charity appeals (*Children in Need*, the Variety Club and *Telethon* on two occasions). The mood of these reports was predictably sympathetic and indeed emotive, with statements such as, 'These children have shown talent and determination in overcoming their disabilities' (*Newsview*, BBC2, 19/11/88), which referred to young deaf and blind people at a *Children in Need* awards ceremony. Other special achievement stories included two reports about the paralympic medal winners returning home and one about Colin Moynihan, the Sports Minister, meeting some athletes with disabilities.

Five of the stories that suggested people with disabilities were courageous also hinted that they were unfortunate. There was no particular pattern evident in these stories. Three were about compensation, two were about the Peto Institute in Budapest and two were about award ceremonies. Table 3.5 indicates the frequencies with which some of these themes did or did not appear in news story-lines.

Of the 11 news stories that mentioned the rights of people with disabilities, 4 were about court battles for compensation and were mostly conveniently categorised as individual (rather than collective) struggles for some sort of equality.

Other stories that fell into this category included two reports quoting new survey statistics about the number of disabled people in the country (Martin, Meltzer and Eliot, 1988) and how these had been grossly underestimated by the Government; a report about AIDS, which included interviews with people who were HIV positive; and a report about the community care system, based on interviews with parents of disabled people who were being forced out of psychiatric hospitals.

The majority of news items that discussed problems faced by people with disabilities due to lack of understanding or the prejudice of other people or society in general were items that also mentioned that disabled people had rights to fight for. Examples of stories that fell into this category were two reports on the controversial television drama *Tumbledown*, in which Jeremy Lawrence, whose story the play told, described how badly he had been treated by the armed forces since being seriously wounded in the Falklands. A story about a new potential cure for exceptionally small children who were unlikely to grow stressed the problems that such children were likely to have in fitting into their peer groups. Two reports about AIDS, in which people with the disease were interviewed, went to some length to criticise the way in which they were treated by others and the level of ignorance that exists about the condition.

News programmes are the single most prevalent genre on peak time television, making up 17 per cent of the programmes coded. Audiences for the main news bulletins are fairly stable at around 8–10 million viewers per channel for the early evening news and 7 million for the mid-evening news. While the news is not a platform for raising and discussing 'issues', concern is expressed from time to time about how reports are presented, what appears on the news and how subjects are treated.

The news stories involving people with disabilities covered a considerable range of subject matter and did from time to time raise issues such as discrimination against people with AIDS, under-funding of institutions for people with special needs and the controversy surrounding the play *Tumbledown*. There did, however, seem to be an exceptionally large number of stories involving disabled children; in fact, of the 52 news stories featuring people with disabilities as a major part of the story, nearly half (24) involved disabled children. A more subjective classification of whether or not the story was emotional or sentimental in any way suggests that over a third (20) of the reports fell into this category. Many of the more emotional reports were in fact about charity appeals or award ceremonies, which made up 12 of the 52 reports.

There were 11 instances in which disabled people were completely incidental to the story and were thus not referred to at all. Examples of such cases were 3 reports about the war in Afghanistan, in which disabled people appeared in the background, and 3 reports from the House of Lords showing a stenographer who was a wheelchair user.

News language

The language used by news presenters and reporters in referring to people with disabilities was categorised for the purposes of the study as neutral, impersonal or derogatory. In 'neutral' language the people in question were referred to by name with no reference to their disabilities, or if disability was mentioned the terms were 'people/ person with a disability' or 'disabled people/person'. 'Impersonal' language covered expressions such as 'the disabled' or 'the handicapped'. 'Derogatory' language would have included terms like 'cripples', 'dummies' and so on, but this never occurred during our sampling period.

Two types of references to people with disabilities that did occur fairly regularly on the news were those saying either how 'brave and plucky' or how 'unfortunate' they were.

The references were not necessarily direct but the stories hinted at the bravery and resilience of the people in question. For example, during a report about a young Lebanese boy who was paralysed and treated at Stoke Mandeville Hospital we heard how he 'still manages a brave smile' and how he is a boy that 'Britain has taken to its heart' (ITV, 21/5/88). Of the 17 stories that were to some extent concerned with the 'courage' of people with disabilities, three-quarters (13) featured or involved children.

While the language used by reporters and presenters referring to people with disabilities was on no occasion coded as slang or derogatory, there did not appear to be any consistent pattern in the terminology used. In over a third of the reports (38.5 per cent) terms such as 'the disabled' or 'the handicapped' were used which, while convenient shorthand, may cause offence.

DOCUMENTARIES

Of the 155 documentaries shown during the six week sampling period, 21 contained people with disabilities. In addition to these a further 7 documentaries containing disability were drawn from outside the sampling period. As with news programmes, the appearance of people with disabilities in documentaries can be broken down by storyline, as in Table 3.6.

Again, the most prevalent types of storyline related to medical issues and the improvement of disabling syndromes. The documentaries in which these issues arose were diverse. They included *The Power of Music* (BBC1, 26/10/88), which featured Paul McCartney discussing the value of music therapy for mentally handicapped people, *Jimmy's* (ITV, 27/10/88), which highlighted the problems faced in coming to terms with a leg amputation, and *Where There's Life* (ITV, 1/6/88), in which a young boy from Hong Kong about to undergo a transplant operation was interviewed and the problems facing donors discussed.

None of the documentaries coded featured stories about people with disabilities achieving special goals such as winning medals in the Paralympics or crossing America in a wheelchair. However, on six occasions the 'achievement' of being able to live relatively normal lives was touched upon. Examples of such documentaries were *If You Love Him Let Him Go* (BBC2, 1/6/88), which looked at two mentally handicapped adults and the pros and cons of letting them live at home with their parents or sending them to special homes. In all

Table 3.6 Types of storyline in documentary programmes including people with disabilities

	Number of reports featuring storyline
Treatment (medical)	8
Rehabilitation	7
Cure/partial cure	6
Normal achievement	6
Tragedy	6
Victim	4
Incidental to the story	4
Struggle for equality	3
Prejudice	2
Other	4

Note: More than one storyline could be coded for each report

cases where this type of storyline was raised it was incidental to the main topics under discussion.

In all cases where disability was viewed as a tragedy in documentaries it was the result of an accident or when able-bodied people became disabled. *World in Action* (ITV, 24/10/88) looked at the injuries sustained by Melinka Heed whilst undergoing a routine appendix operation, and the resulting fight for compensation. *Brass Tacks* (BBC2, 17/5/88) featured an investigation into the attitude of the army toward people injured and disabled during military training, and *Viewpoint '88* (ITV, 17/5/88) showed a documentary made by a reporter who had sustained injuries during an assassination attempt in South Africa.

In only four documentaries was the prejudice suffered by people with disabilities or the struggle for equality brought up. In the previously mentioned *World in Action* (ITV, 24/10/88) programme this struggle took the form of compensation for injuries sustained and did not discuss any broader issues relating to rights and equality. Of the other three programmes, two related to people with AIDS, *Facing up to AIDS* (BBC2, 26/10/88) and *AIDS: A Priest's Testament* (Channel 4, 5/10/88), both of which focused some attention on the discrimination faced by AIDS sufferers. The other programme, *Reid About Russia* (Channel 4, 4/6/88), featured a brief discussion with a controversial Russian film-maker who had recently completed a film about the conflict in Afghanistan. A clip shown from the film discussed how the Soviet Government and Soviet society treated people injured and disabled in the war, trying to hide them away and to forget about them.

In several documentaries people with disabilities were referred to as, or implied to be, brave, courageous, plucky or unfortunate. In most cases this was implicit rather than explicit. However, in one instance, *I Want to Live* (BBC2, 27/10/88), a woman's fight against cancer which is surprising medical experts was looked at, as was the way in which her will to live helped her to fight the illness. In this programme the courageous battle against cancer featured heavily.

In most cases disability in documentaries was discussed in a detached and unemotional way. In only 4 of the 28 programmes was the report in any way emotional or sentimental. One of these programmes was an appeal on behalf of a hospice, *Lifeline* (BBC1, 30/10/88); the other three were the already mentioned *40 Minutes* programme *I Want to Live* (BBC2, 27/10/88), *Where There's Life* (ITV, 1/6/88) and *The Power of Music* (BBC1, 26/10/88).

OTHER NON-FICTION PROGRAMMES

Of the 128 factual programmes coded that portrayed or discussed disability during the sampling period, nearly two-thirds (59 per cent) were either news, documentaries or current affairs programmes. The remainder (53 programmes) were mostly magazine programmes. An analysis of the main storylines in these 53 programmes reveals that the most commonly presented was the special achievement of people with disabilities.

Overall, one-quarter (25 per cent) of these programmes were to some extent concerned with the special achievements of people with disabilities. Of these, well over half (62 per cent) were concerned with charity (8 programmes) and featured footage from the Paralympics in Seoul. In some instances people with disabilities were shown in a fairly neutral light and praised solely for their achievements rather than for having reached such heights with a disability. Probably the best examples were two of the reports of the Paralympics, both of which appeared on ITV's regional magazine programmes. These served to congratulate participants for winning medals (Central Post, 28/10/88, *Central News*, 28/10/88). The other two reports about the Paralympics went to some length to praise the courage and fortitude of the competitors (*Midlands Today*, 25/10/88, *Central News*, 27/10/88). Three other special achievement stories appeared on regional magazine programmes and these all featured charity appeals. One

Table 3.7 Types of storyline in 'other non-fiction programmes' including people with disabilities

	Frequency	Percentage of total	Proportion of programmes with storyline
Special achievement	13	18	25%
Normal achievement	9	13	17%
Struggle for equality	8	11	15%
Treatment (medical)	7	10	13%
Tragedy	6	8	11%
Rehabilitation	5	7	9%
Cure	4	6	8%
Prejudice	4	6	8%
Other	16	22	30%
Total	72	101	

Note: Based on 53 programmes covering 72 identifiable storylines reported on how money from the 1987 *Children in Need* appeal had been spent in the Midlands (*Midlands Today*, 15/11/88). Another reported how a woman with a few weeks to live was spending her time raising money (*Central Weekend*, 28/10/88) and one featured an amputee who regularly ran marathons and had just been awarded a man of the year medal (*Central News*, 9/11/88).

Other programmes seemed to be specifically about charities or good deeds. *Hearts of Gold*, which occurred twice (BBC1, 5/11/88, 19/11/88), is a programme presented by Esther Rantzen that applauds such good deeds. Two programmes coded highlighted a man who is blind and has set up a club for the lonely in London, a pop group which raised money for a cancer-screening machine and a policeman active in disability charity work. Another charity pro- gramme, *Lifeline* (BBC, 5/6/88), included a charity appeal on behalf of a centre for children with cerebral palsy.

Two further programmes praising the achievements of people with disabilities are worth mentioning, *Children of Courage* (BBC1, 18/11/88) and *SOS Star Awards* (BBC1, 30/5/88). *Children of Courage* was part of the *Children in Need* appeal, and was a programme devoted to 'children who have shown courage in the face of adversity, either by helping others or by overcoming personal difficulties'. The *SOS Star Awards* (Stars Organisation for Spastics) were presented by Noel Edmonds to 'somebody who has overcome their handicap ... or someone who helps others overcome their handicaps'. The pro- gramme emphasised overcoming disabilities and was suffused with praise for special achievements. There was no mention of other issues connected with being disabled and the general atmosphere of the programme was one of both sympathy and congratulation.

There were 9 programmes in which stories were shown that to varying extents mentioned some sort of struggle for equality or the prejudice suffered by people with disabilities. Three of these were *Listening Eye*, a programme produced and presented by people with disabilities, each of which covered several topics relating to the struggle for equality for people with disabilities. Three regional magazine programmes also briefly looked at such issues. Two of these reported on the medal winners in the Seoul Paralympics and questioned the lack of coverage of the games (*Central News*, 27/10/88, *Midlands Today*, 25/10/88). The third (*Central Weekend*, 27/5/88) featured an interview and discussion with Charles Wood, the playwright who wrote *Tumbledown*, in which he complained about the armed forces' poor treatment of Falklands' war veterans who were injured in the conflict.

The final three programmes that touched on disability issues were *Points of View* (BBC1, 18/5/88), which featured a complaint about the lack of sub-titles on television, *First Tuesday* (ITV, 1/11/88), which discussed the lack of adequate facilities for dyslexic children, and *The Media Show*, which screened a lively debate about *Telethon*, arguing that it was insulting to people with disabilities. This report was a rare opportunity for people with disabilities to voice an opinion about television output on a mainstream programme. The prevailing sentiment among those participating in the programme was that *Telethon* put over a very negative view and that people with disabilities should not have to rely upon charity to meet their needs. There were of course voices in opposition to this view, for example, 'programmes such as *Telethon* should be encouraged as much as possible, mainly because people really enjoy being able to give, and it's great fun' (Edwina Currie).

Language used in other non-fiction programmes

The type of language used by presenters in non-fiction programmes other than news and documentaries, when referring to people with disabilities, was also examined.

As with news programmes, there were evidently no clear guidelines for the use of language other than to avoid obviously derogatory terminology. The one instance of clearly offensive language occurred on *Wogan* (BBC1, 28/10/88) during an interview with Mike Smith and Sarah Green shortly after they had survived a helicopter crash. Mike Smith was describing amusing moments which they had experienced since being temporarily disabled: 'there was this hilarious sight of these two cripples struggling across the pavement'.

In over half of the 53 programmes the reports featuring people with disabilities touched on the physical problems of living with a disability (see Table 3.8). For example, in the previously mentioned *Wogan* interview with Sarah Green and Mike Smith their mobility and access problems due to their injuries were discussed. They mentioned how this had highlighted for them the need for easier access to buildings and general considerations in relation to planning and building for people with limited mobility.

The programmes that mentioned equality for people with

Table 3.8 Types of issue raised in non-fiction programmes

	Frequency	Proportion of programmes
Physical problems of being disabled	27	51%
Lack of understanding by society/individuals	17	32%
Rights to fight for	13	25%

Note: More than one could be coded for each programme

disabilities and acknowledged in some way that there were issues here to be discussed tended to be the same programmes that talked about the failure or refusal of individuals and society in general to understand or acknowledge these issues. In most cases such discussions were brief and limited, as in the previously mentioned *Wogan* episode in which a few sentences dealt with problems of access faced by people with locomotion difficulties and the lack of any apparent progress to improve matters.

The programmes which looked most closely at issues relating to equality for people with disabilities were two episodes of *Same Difference* – a programme made specifically for them. The only other programmes that went into any detail about related issues were: *The Media Show* (Channel 4, 20/11/88), which, as previously mentioned, discussed the portrayal of people with disabilities on *Telethon*; *First Tuesday* (ITV, 1/11/88), which discussed the treatment of dyslexic children in schools; and *Where There's Life* (ITV, 6/7/88), which discussed the rights of people who had had a stroke to dictate their own method, speed and goals of recovery.

Unlike news programmes, which featured a large number of stories about children with disabilities, only 9 (17 per cent) of the magazine and other factual programmes that showed people with disabilities ran reports involving children. There was also less of a tendency to report in an emotional way stories involving people with disabilities. Only 8 (15.1 per cent) were so presented. Five of these involved charity appeals; one looked at young children at the Peto Institute in Budapest (*Midlands Today*, BBC1, 2/6/88); *That's Life* (BBC1, 22/5/88) talked to young children involved in transplant operations; and a report on *Central News* and *Magazine* (ITV,

23/5/88) talked to young children in a cancer ward, the sentimentality of this story being summed up by the reporter in his closing lines: 'What a marvellous story. It gives you real hope.'

As a footnote to this section it is worth briefly mentioning quiz and game shows. On not one of the 48 quiz and game shows coded did any people with disabilities appear, and the only mention of disability came up in *Connections* (ITV, 24/5/88); in this programme contestants are allowed to donate money to a charity of their choice and on this occasion the money was given to a trust to provide homes and further education for mentally handicapped adults.

Chapter 4

The portrayal of disability in fictional programmes

In this chapter we will be concerned with the ways in which disabled people are represented in fictional programmes. Let us briefly outline the reasons why this is important.

In Chapter 1 we noted that there is a substantial normative element in the definition of disability: that is, our ideas about disability reflect what we believe people should properly be able to do. While we are mindful of the suffering and hardship which disability may bring, there is an undeniable social dimension to the issue, in the definition of what disability is, in the attitudes and beliefs which the able-bodied hold about disabled people and, more importantly for the present chapter, in how predominantly able-bodied decision-makers in television and film organisations represent and use disability in their productions.

We are trying to deal with the meaning of programmes rather than the features which can most easily be coded. Whereas we cannot, for example, say with certainty how the quality of 'sentimentality' could be coded with high intersubjective consistency, we can begin to delineate some of its features. Our ambitions in this chapter tie in with some of the debates about disability on television. We are dealing with some of the features which disability activists themselves identify as significant, for example, the theme of individual courage in the face of adversity and the supposedly sentimental way in which disabled people are often represented.

Many of the programmes discussed here are films, which suggests that this chapter is not entirely about television, but some of these, as we shall see, are films made for television, and films do comprise a substantial part of television programming.

Fiction is an important part of popular culture. In this chapter we are accepting the anthropological assumption that an important resource for understanding a culture is its entertainment forms. Fiction, particularly when it is popular, can suggest the sorts of things which people are interested in and can reflect the way in which they think. The history of literature and entertainment suggests that fictional forms are an important vehicle for the representation of life, and that the techniques and repertoires of representation carry some meaning about the way in which people in that society conceptualise and deal with everyday existence.

Finally, we want to give a richer picture of how disabled people were represented in the programmes which we sampled than the earlier chapters have so far presented.

In this chapter, then, we shall be examining the repertoires of representation and looking at the functions which they perform in the construction of a view of disability. This work is not definitive, but represents more a series of suggestions about how such an analysis might proceed. However, in the light of some scholars' recent interest in the analysis of discourse and the elucidation of meaning from cultural forms, it is important to provide some commentary on how this approach might proceed.

QUANTITATIVE OVERVIEW OF DRAMATIC FICTION

Nearly one-third (31 per cent) of the 1,286 programmes coded during the six week sampling period fell into the various dramatic fiction categories. Dramatic fiction as defined in this section excluded comedy sketches, light entertainment such as game shows, cartoons and children's television, other than children's drama. In this sample, as Table 4.1 shows, BBC1 showed the most dramatic fiction (131 programmes), followed by ITV (113 programmes), Channel 4 (102 programmes) and BBC2 (58 programmes).

Overall less than one in five programmes (19 per cent) had any characters with an identifiable disability.

Channel differences were small: BBC2 had the highest proportion of programmes in which disability was portrayed (21 per cent), compared with 20 per cent of both ITV and Channel 4 programmes and 17 per cent of BBC1 drama programmes. It must be remembered that a programme would be coded as portraying disability no matter what role was played by a disabled character. Thus, included in these

Table 4.1 Number of dramatic fiction programmes portraying disability, by channel

Disability portrayed?	Channel									
	BBC1 Number %		BBC2 Number %		ITV Number %		C4 Number %		Total Number %	
Yes	22	17	12	21	23	20	20	20	77	19
No	109	83	46	79	90	80	82	80	327	81
Total	131	100	58	100	113	100	102	100	404	100

figures are programmes that showed disabled characters only fleetingly in background or incidental roles.

ROLE IMPORTANCE

All characters, including the disabled, were categorised according to their importance in the production. Four categories were used: *major*, *minor*, *incidental* and *background*. Characters were coded as *incidental* if they appeared briefly, had few lines and were not integral to the plot. These were distinguished from *background* characters in non-speaking roles who appeared as fill-in characters.

It is difficult to discuss the function and role of disabled people in dramatic fiction without some speculation about the meanings which they will have for the audience and the intentions and motives of the production team, yet we have no audience or production data which corresponds directly to this content analysis. However, perhaps we can suggest some of the connotations which depictions of disabled people might have. For example, an incidental role in the 'spaghetti western' *The Good, the Bad and the Ugly* (BBC2, 28/8/88) was filled by a disabled character. During the opening shots of the film one of the major characters, played by Lee Van Cleef, is informed about the whereabouts and activities of an old adversary by a man with no legs who is referred to as 'Half Soldier'. The role is limited to a few lines and 'Half Soldier' appears only once.

From this portrayal we can perhaps suggest that the term 'Half Soldier' indicates that in the film people missing limbs are considered to be less than fully human. Maybe the incapacity of 'Half Soldier' contrasts with the physical excellence of the character played by Van Cleef, whose marksmanship is a feature of the series of films of which *The Good, the Bad and the Ugly* is a part. Perhaps the portrayal is intended to suggest the harshness and lack of compassion in nineteenth-century American life, in which case the film is conveying the emotional tone of the period. The harshness which the film constructs may be contrasted with other possibilities which it does not present, such as a version of the 'life was hard but the people were kind' account of history.

An example of a background role occurred in *Under Fire* (ITV, 24/9/88), a film about a photographer in a Central American civil war. In one scene the photographer is seen approaching a village from which about 20 people are fleeing, presumably to escape the fighting. One of these characters is seen propelling himself in a wheelchair. The shot lasts less than 10 seconds and no verbal reference is made to the disabled character. Again, we can suggest some of the meanings conveyed by this scene: that the war did not respect vulnerable civilian life; that the man had to propel himself, because under fire people act selfishly. Other possibilities are excluded by this depiction, such as the practice of mutual support in adversity.

Thus, even very brief depictions of disability can suggest certain models of human nature, of history, of emotion, and exclude others. We cannot definitively identify the narrative function of disability, but it remains difficult to escape the implications which cohere around it concerning human nature or the nature of the historical setting.

Overall one half (51 per cent) of all the disabled characters were portrayed only fleetingly in background roles.

Of course, in many dramatic productions background characters are likely to constitute the majority of people appearing. Unfortunately, with large crowd scenes, the total numbers of background characters cannot be estimated with much accuracy. Thus, while a

Table 4.2 Role importance of disabled characters in dramatic fiction

Role importance	Number	Percentage
Major role	38	21
Minor role	28	15
Incidental role	24	13
Background only	92	51
Total	182	100

Table 4.3 Comparative frequency of disabled and non-disabled
characters in dramatic fiction

Role importance	Disabled Number	Percentage	Non-disabled Number	Percentage
Major role	38	(42)	2431	(36)
Minor role	28	(31)	2270	(33)
Incidental role	24	(27)	2120	(31)
Total	90	(100)	6821	(100)

Table 4.4 Disabled characters as a proportion of all characters in
dramatic fiction, by role importance

Role importance	Number of disabled characters	Number of characters	Proportion disabled Percentage
Major role	38	2469	1.5
Minor role	28	2298	1.2
Incidental role	24	2144	1.1
Total	90	6911	1.3

count was attempted of all these, the number estimated (nearly
29,000) is only an approximation of the actual number. Far more
reliable counts can be obtained of incidental characters (who had
speaking parts) and of those in major and minor roles. In order to
compare the relative frequency of disabled and non-disabled
characters only these roles will be examined (see Table 4.3).

The relative frequency of the various roles does not differ very
much between disabled and non-disabled characters. However, Table
4.3 indicates very clearly how infrequently disabled characters
appeared. Overall, disabled characters make up only 1.3 per cent of
all those portrayed on television who have a speaking part. The
proportions for each category of role importance are presented in
Table 4.4.

Although disabled characters are somewhat better represented
among major roles than elsewhere, even here they make up only 1.5
per cent of the leading parts in dramatic fiction.

DISABILITY AND GENRE OF DRAMATIC PROGRAMME

As might be expected the largest categories of programme by genre are soap operas, situation comedies and 'other dramas' (drama programmes that do not fit into any of the defined categories). Each of these contributed one in four dramatic fiction programmes to our sample.

What stands out in our analysis is the low percentage of both soap operas (8 per cent) and situation comedies (9 per cent) portraying people with disabilities. In some ways this is surprising. Soap operas – at least British ones – have regularly been a platform from which social problems and to some extent political issues have been aired. Recent examples on *Eastenders* and *Brookside* include drug and alcohol abuse, homosexuality, AIDS, rape, racism, one parent families, abortion, domestic violence and divorce. During our six week sampling period only 8 soap opera episodes touched on disability (8 per cent of all soaps). Four of these episodes occurred in the Australian series *Neighbours*, and three dealt with a temporary disability (Mrs Mangel fell off a ladder and hit her head, suffering memory loss and some confusion). The fourth concerned an escapee from a secure mental hospital who kidnapped Helen Daniels. In neither of these instances was mental illness dealt with seriously: Mrs Mangel's disorientation appeared to be a part of the embarrassment she regularly suffers and the mental hospital escapee's problems were presented as something exotic, disturbing and alien. Perhaps then the mental problems were dramatic devices rather than serious attempts to deal with the issue of mental difficulties.

A further three cases occurred in *Emmerdale Farm*: Annie, a 65-year-old, had recently received a hip operation. As a result of this she was prescribed tranquillisers and appeared to be generally disorientated. Although this was a more serious study of a disability issue, the thrust of the scenes was not disability as such but the effect of tranquillisers and tranquilliser dependency. More recently in *Eastenders*, the character Colin suffered ill health for some time and then discovered that he had multiple sclerosis, but the potential to investigate some of the issues surrounding the disability was lost when he was written out of the series.

Situation comedies, unlike soap operas, rarely involve social or political issues. 'Sitcoms' more regularly draw from a restricted repertoire of stereotypes and the potential for dealing sensitively with issues must compete with the imperative of gaining laughs. Less than one in ten (9 per cent) of the 94 'sit coms' recorded during the sampling period portrayed any characters with disabilities. Despite the small sample of disabled characters, situation comedies such as *Fawlty Towers*, *'Allo 'Allo* and *Blackadder* appeared to use disability as a humorous device rather than as an opportunity to deal with the experience of being disabled or the way in which society treats disabled people. The following examples illustrate the style of these.

In *Fawlty Towers* (BBC1, 9/11/88) a hearing-impaired character, Mrs Richards, came to stay at the hotel run by Basil Fawlty, played by John Cleese. The programme was peppered with misunderstandings on her part due to her hearing aid malfunctioning, causing Basil Fawlty to become frustrated and predictably rude. On arriving in her room Mrs Richards complains that the bath is too small and the view unsatisfactory. She adds, 'And what's more the radio doesn't work.' The radio does in fact work but she cannot hear it because her hearing aid is not working. 'No, the radio works, you don't', replies Basil and then he calls her a 'scabby old battle axe' in a hushed voice. Later Basil walks up to Mrs Richards to say something to her, but before speaking, shouts 'Testing, testing....' Towards the end of the episode, when she has her hearing aid turned on, Basil pretends to talk to her, silently moving his lips; so she turns her hearing aid up to maximum volume, at which point Basil shouts into the microphone. Thus, Mrs Richards's problems and Basil's responses to them are presented as jokes. Mrs Richards is the oddity whose anomalous properties cause frustration. It is perhaps arguable whether the programme invites us to laugh at her or at Basil's impatient and prejudiced response, but it is her presence which introduces the humour into the situation.

Other episodes also made disability the butt of jokes. For example, 'the Major' is a regular character in the series. Elderly and a little deaf, he often misunderstands what people are saying to him; grasping the wrong end of the stick provides the humour of many scenes in which he is featured.

However, disabled characters in situation comedies are not invariably treated in a negative way. In an episode of *Help* (BBC1, 15/5/89), one of the characters was waiting for her childhood sweetheart to return from sea. Eventually he arrives, disabled by the loss of one arm. Interestingly, this disability seemed to be quite irrelevant to the relationship or indeed the plot. This was one of the few occasions when disability was presented as a matter-of-fact normality. Another example of a more positive portrayal of a character with a disability was in the *Return of Shelley* (ITV, 1/11/88).[1] In this episode Shelley is celebrating his birthday in a wine bar when a man in a wheelchair arrives. The manager objects to the wheelchair, making excuses about 'fire regulations' in order to throw Dave, the disabled character, out. Shelley intervenes to question the manager's decision – 'when did you last hear of wheelchairs exploding spontaneously?' he asks. After some discussion Shelley announces, 'If he goes, I go', and they leave together to continue celebrating. This is unusual in that the central character displays solidarity with the disabled person, who turns out to share Shelley's penchant for wit. Thus, in this respect the disabled person shares the valued characteristics of the hero, and the narrative appears to suggest that the landlord is unlike the pair of them, and therefore less important and less likely to be in the right.

Apart from soap operas, situation comedies and films there were only 30 other dramatic fiction programmes during the sampling period that included a portrayal of disability. Half of these (15) were shown on ITV; 8 on BBC1; 3 on BBC2 and 4 on Channel 4. Of these 30 programmes, the minority (12) were home-produced. Most (16) were US productions and the other two Australian. Overall, 22 of the programmes portrayed disabled characters in either major or minor roles.

The majority of these programmes (13) were either police or detective programmes (9 of which were US productions). A further 6 were hospital or medical dramas and 2 were children's dramas. Although the sample size is too small to draw confident conclusions, it is interesting to note that of the 30 programmes over half (16) had disabled characters in more than one episode. *St Elsewhere* (Channel 4, 24/5/88, 31/5/88, 25/10/88) had 3 episodes portraying disabled characters. *LA Law* on ITV had 3 episodes featuring disabled characters (ITV, 12/5/88, 19/5/88, 2/6/88) out of 4 episodes coded. *Legwork*, an American series about a young lawyer, portrayed disabled characters in both episodes coded (ITV, 13/5/88, 20/5/88). *The Equalizer*, coded three times during the sampling period, portrayed characters with disabilities on all three occasions (ITV, 25/5/88, 27/10/88, 16/11/88). *Rockliffe's Babies, Beauty and the Beast* and *The Singing Detective* featured disability in more than one episode – the latter in all.

In 5 of these 30 programmes the disabled characters were portrayed as criminals, in 9 programmes the disabled characters were shown as victims or people suffering, in a further 9 programmes they were either background or incidental characters, and the other 7 programmes had disabled characters in other more general roles.

During the sampling period three episodes of *The Equalizer* were coded, but it is worth mentioning here a further two episodes drawn from outside the sampling period (ITV, 8/6/88, 22/9/88). Plots in the series concern the work of a tough private detective who stands up for the oppressed and helpless. In one of the five episodes a disabled character briefly appears as a background character and plays no part in the storyline of the programme. In the other four episodes, however, the disabled characters play central roles. In three of the episodes the disabled characters are victims who need The Equalizer's help and sense of social justice to get them out of their various predicaments. In the fourth episode a psychopath is on the loose killing middle-aged women. The Equalizer shows true compassion and understanding toward the killer, saving him from prison and ensuring his referral to a mental institution for psychiatric treatment.

The police series *Rockliffe's Babies* was coded four times during the sampling period and on two occasions characters with disabilities appeared (BBC1, 13/5/88, 3/6/88). The general theme of *Rockliffe's Babies* is the day-to-day operations of a team of young police officers under the watchful and cynical eye of their Chief, Rockliffe. Their operations rarely go smoothly and the inexperience of the officers is essential to the humour in the series. Both episodes contained both minor and incidental disabled characters. In one the minor character was a slow-learning boy who disappears and is later found dead. He is referred to by the police and public as 'the Dumbo'. Perhaps the programme is trying to capture the prejudicial terminology found in everyday life, but the use of the term is not significantly disputed in the programme. The second episode showed a nervous, drug-addicted bank robber who is labelled by the police as mentally ill. However, a noticeable similarity between the two episodes was in the incidental characters. On both occasions the police give chase to criminals who have just carried out robberies. In one instance their way is hampered by a woman in a wheelchair and in the other the road is blocked by an invalid carriage. Whereas we cannot make any comment about the series as a whole, these last two instances seem to be associating disability with hindrance and obstruction. Moreover, it is the police whom they obstruct rather than the criminals, so it is almost as if the disabled people are interfering with the proper running of society. Whereas the intentions of the programme-makers might be impeccable, the difficulties which disabled people face in being accepted as competent, useful members of society suggest that we should question this kind of depiction.

Another programme that portrayed disabled characters in more than one episode was *St Elsewhere* (Channel 4, 24/3/88, 31/5/88, 28/19/88). As this series is set in a hospital, it is perhaps not surprising that disabled characters appeared regularly. *LA Law* featured disabled characters in 3 out of 4 episodes coded during the sampling period (ITV, 12/5/88, 19/5/88, 2/6/88). In this instance the characters had quite different roles. In one episode a pregnant woman is dying of leukaemia. This raised ethical and legal issues as to whether or not she should be forced to have a potentially lethal Caesarean operation in order to ensure the baby's survival. One episode portrayed a colourful eccentric who has become obsessed with a character he once played in the movies and now runs around Los Angeles dressed in Batman style clothes. The court threatens to commit him to a mental institution and the law firm defends him. One other episode showed the plight of a mentally handicapped employee of the law firm. The employee, Ben, makes a costly mistake which a colleague attempts to cover up in order to protect him. Despite his vulnerability, Ben admits to his mistake, thus retaining his integrity but also increasing awareness in others of his limitations as an employee.

The portrayals of disabled characters in *LA Law* seemed to avoid some of the more obvious stereotypes and sentimentality. Nevertheless, the disabled characters were still represented as special cases and seemed to be included only because of their disabilities. In a sense, all their activities are facets of their disability, rather than facets of their nature. Disabled characters portrayed as ordinary people who happen to have disabilities were rare. One of the few exceptions was the detective series *Call Me Mister*, two episodes of which were selected from outside the sampling period (BBC1, 13/8/88, 27/8/88). In this series the head of a detective agency is a wheelchair user. Although reminiscent of the well-known detective Ironside, he is not blessed with Ironside's deductive powers, and *Call Me Mister* did not highlight any social or physical problems connected with disablement although it showed some of the everyday difficulties of access. This is, however, one of the few instances in which a disabled character's role could equally easily have been that of a non-disabled character without threatening the plot.

FILMS

Early in this research it became evident that films were far more likely to include portrayals of disability than other types of production. This impression was confirmed by later analysis: compared with dramatic fiction as a whole, films were twice as likely to include disabled characters. For this reason a further 59 films of special interest to the project were recorded and coded. From the total of 134 films coded, 75 from the sampling period plus 59 additional films, 82 were feature films and 52 were films made for television. Over half of the films in the final sample contained disabled characters. The random sample yielded 75 films of which 27 portrayed characters with disabilities. The boosted sample of special interest films provided an extra 57 disabled characters.

In total, 84 disabled characters in major or minor roles appeared in all 134 films coded. Of these, the majority (55 per cent) were classified as having a physical disability and 24 per cent as mentally ill. As was true of most disabled characters on television, a large proportion of the disabilities were severe. For example, one-quarter (25 per cent) of the physically disabled characters could not work at all and an equal number (26 per cent) used wheelchairs.

As Table 4.5 shows, just over half (51 per cent) of the major and minor disabled characters coded fell into the 'other drama' genre category, that is, drama which could not be categorised more

Table 4.5 Number of major and minor disabled characters in films, by genre

Genre	No. of disabled characters	Percentage of disabled characters
Crime	5	6
Thriller	10	12
Spy	1	1
Western	1	1
War	11	13
Historical drama	2	2
Other drama	43	51
Horror	3	4
Avant-garde	1	1
Comedy	4	5
Fantasy	3	4
Total	84	100

specifically, 18 per cent appeared in crime or thriller films and 13 per cent in war films. Only 9 war films were shown, but this genre had the highest density of disabled characters, largely due to one film, *Coming Home* (Channel 4, 22/7/88), which featured 8 major and minor disabled characters.

Of the 72 films portraying disabled characters, 19 had only background or incidental characters with disabilities. These 19 films did not discuss or investigate any issues relating to disability. However, out of the remaining 53 films with major and minor disabled characters, just under half (25) examined or discussed some issue relating to disability. Of these 25 films, 9 were UK-produced, 15 were US-produced and one was an Australian production.

The issues examined, although approached in a variety of ways, can be conveniently categorised into six subject areas (see Table 4.6). In 8 of the films prejudice and the rights of people with disabilities to make their own decisions were examined, 6 films looked at special achievements of people with disabilities, 5 looked at rehabilitation or coming to terms with disability, 3 provided some sort of description of a disability and how it develops and affects people over time, one film looked specifically at the treatment of a disability and one film, *Whose Life is it Anyway?* (BBC2, 14/9/88), fitted several categories. See Table 4.6, in which a conspicuous theme of achievement describes the fairly simple storyline of 6 of the films.

Ice Castles (Channel 4, 29/8/88) is a film about a girl aspiring to become an Olympic ice-dancer. During an unsupervised practice session she falls, badly injuring her head and hence losing her sight. After the accident she becomes bitter, rejecting the people close to her and her previous life style, convinced that her ambitions have been destroyed. However, with the dedicated encouragement of her parents, her trainer and her boyfriend she finally returns to competitive skating.

In *Ice Castles* overcoming the handicap of disability is an all or nothing affair judged in terms of the triumph of winning a competition. The mundane reality of day-to-day problems receives scant attention. In this the film is reminiscent of the story of Douglas Bader in *Reach for the Sky* (Channel 4, 14/9/88), whose trauma at losing both legs and the reaction of other people to this are lost as issues in his heroic struggle to return to life as he had enjoyed it. Before his accident, we are constantly reminded of Bader's active life – 'He may even be chosen for the England Rugger Squad this year' –

Table 4.6 Main themes of films dealing with issues relating to disability

Title	Channel	Date shown	Main theme	Other themes
The Sender	1	10.05.88	R	T
The Best Little Girl in the World	4	16.05.88	DD	
Tumbledown	1	31.05.88	P	R
Family Life	4	03.06.88	P	T
Do You Remember Love?	2	04.07.88	DD	CT
The Terry Fox Story	1	05.07.88	A	R
Catherine	3	12.07.88	DD	
Coming Home	4	22.07.88	R	P
Who'll Love My Children?	1	24.07.88	CT	
23 Paces to Baker Street	1	29.07.88	A	R
Ice Castles	4	29.08.88	A	R
Promise	1	08.09.88	DD	
Champion	3	14.09.88	A	T
Reach for the Sky	4	14.09.88	A	R
Whose Life is it Anyway?	2	14.09.88	T	
Beg, Borrow or Steal	3	16.09.88	P	A
Urge to Kill	4	23.09.88	P	
Touched by Love	1	30.09.88	T	
Deer Hunter	2	02.10.88	R	
A Shining Season	4	10.10.88	A	CT
Bill	4	17.10.88	P	DD
Annie's Coming Out	2	31.10.88	P	
Committed	4	07.11.88	P	
Sentimental Journey	4	07.11.88	R	
The Man Upstairs	4	15.11.88	P	

Key
A = Achievement   P = Prejudice
CT = Coming to terms   R = Rehabilitation
DD = Describing disability T = Treatment

and his daredevil attitude to life. After the accident, there is a brief spell of rehabilitation and then the glory of heroically overcoming the disability and returning to active service in the Royal Air Force.

In discussing the themes within films of this kind it is appropriate to deal with the issue of sentimentality. We have already noted that there seem to be some consistent themes running through many of them, such as heroism, achievement and the indomitable spirit of those who triumph over adversity. We might characterise the atmosphere in such films as 'sentimental'. This immediately invites some very complex issues regarding the origin of emotions, and takes us away from visual or soundtrack features which can be coded with a high degree of consistency. However, the kinds of emotion which the film seems to encourage are important in understanding the potential ways in which an audience might interpret it. It is also important for us to begin to characterise some of the features which construct this sense of emotion. Critics of content analysis often suggest that it is incapable of capturing argument, narrative or emotion, but we have very little other than intuition with which to identify these features. Why do our 'heartstrings' feel pulled? We might try to look for correspondences between the situations where people experience certain kinds of emotion in society at large and in films, but this does not answer the question of how films come to evoke emotions.

It is instructive to examine what the films tend not to emphasise. We very rarely see the topic of disability introduced as a social issue. The customary highly individualistic struggle masks the possibility that disability results not only from an individual's limitations but also from an environment which is designed with only able-bodied people in mind. There are strong suggestions in many films that disability is about courage and achievement rather than suggesting that it is an issue for which society as a whole should take responsibility.

The theme of sentiment mentioned above emerges in a slightly different form when we consider the issues of terminal illness and degenerative conditions. Rather than a sense of recovery and achievement, we have a constructed sense of impending death. Again, the precise mechanisms whereby this sense is achieved are enigmatic and evade precise analysis. Films of this type include *Sentimental Journey* (Channel 4, 7/11/88), about a woman coping with a terminal heart condition, *Do You Remember Love?* (BBC2, 4/7/88), about a woman with Alzheimer's disease, and *Who'll Love My Children?* (BBC1, 24/7/88), about a woman dying of cancer and trying to find homes for her children. In fact, of the 25 films coded that actually probed some issue relating to disability, over half (13) were judged as being to some degree 'sentimental' in their approach and likely to leave the audience feeling sorry for the disabled characters.

Of course, inferring this quality is problematic since we cannot achieve a precise definition of it. Instead we are relying on our intuition that emotions were somehow present. Yet this does not guarantee that the emotion was encoded in the film so much as that we inhabit the same culture of emotions as the production team. The films evoke a highly specific set of emotions, inducing us to feel how sad it is that the person is disabled or dying. It is interesting that there was little done to evoke anger at how the disabled were treated, yet surely this would push the message home just as strongly as the 'tender' emotions which are generally aroused around disability.

A recent example which, while not directly related to disability, illustrates the emotional content of films is *The Accused*. This concerns a woman who was gang raped and her struggle for justice. By showing her struggle and her trauma the film is able to make us feel anger or, perhaps just as importantly, to make us aware that we are being encouraged to feel anger. In this sense emotions are value judgements and are contingent on assessments within a moral order. We are reminded of some set of proper standards concerning human dignity and how people should treat each other. It is the violation of these which induces what we call outrage or anger. In *The Accused* the controversial rape scene might also generate this kind of disapprobation; the camaraderie and obvious enjoyment on the part of the rapists appear particularly reprehensible. In the end convictions are secured against the rapists and thus the highly individualistic message of triumph and inner strength is also secured. In common with films dealing with disability *The Accused* presents very little social or political context so that the position of women or the disabled in society is largely unexamined. *The Accused* and the disability films are in some ways quite conservative, with the former presenting a form of justice based on retribution rather than rehabilitation and a model of male sexuality based on a kind of hydraulic inevitability. A similar pessimism pervades even the most triumphant disability films, in that they offer little alternative to an admiration of inner strength, stoicism and achievement.

Perhaps the most interesting types of storylines were those that discussed prejudice shown towards people with disabilities. The approaches used in different films, the areas concentrated on and the end results varied from film to film. Some, such as *Urge to Kill* (Channel 4, 23/9/88), in which a mentally handicapped young man is accused of murder, used disability within a wider storyline. The same was true of *Beg, Borrow or Steal* (ITV, 16/9/88), in which a group of physically disabled men, frustrated by attempts to raise the capital to open a launderette, plan and carry out a robbery. Other films, such as *Committed* (Channel 4, 7/11/88), an account of Frances Farmer's life story and her committal to a mental hospital, concentrated on the character, who may have been mentally ill, issues immediately surrounding her condition and people's attitudes towards her mental illness in general.

The use of the medium of film to highlight some of the problems faced by disabled people was relatively rare. In 21 per cent of cases the role played by the disabled character in some way reflected aspects of prejudice, negative attitudes or physical problems forced on disabled people. An example of such instances occurred in *Urge to Kill*, mentioned above, in which Hughie, a mentally handicapped young man, is accused of murdering a young woman. The film highlights the prejudiced attitudes of the local population, who immediately blame Hughie with scant circumstantial evidence. The ostensible reason for this is that they do not understand him, are afraid of him and also need a scapegoat for their anger and frustration. In cases such as the above, negative attitudes were directed against the disabled characters by able-bodied characters, apparently in order to make a point about discrimination and prejudice.

It is almost as if the beliefs of the local people are shown to be false and absurd, suggesting that prejudice is irrational; that is, a quite simple model of prejudice as false belief is implied, rather than, for example, institutional prejudice, prejudice which is bound up in common sense or prejudice which invades medical definitions of disability.

In a number of films disabled characters were treated in such a manner without any obvious narrative message. For example, in *Blazing Saddles*, one of the characters, Mungo, is portrayed as being a slow learner, and as a result is kept chained up like a dog and sporadically beaten. This cruelty does not seem to be used to make a point about extreme prejudice; rather it seems to function as a comedy device. In *Don Juan* (Channel 4, 20/5/88) the King of Spain has a court jester who is a dwarf, and the jester is the only person allowed to mock the King. However, the reason for this appears not to be respect, but because he is not taken seriously by the King and has the status equivalent to that of a naughty child. Similar attitudes were shown in 5 of the films coded, although negative attitudes were shown in several other films in which discrimination and prejudice were important issues under examination.

Deciding whether the portrayal of a disabled character is positive or negative is extremely difficult. Whereas many films try to build up a sense of character, it is also true that they cannot cover all aspects of a character's existence and experience. While most films purport to show us reality, it is also true that we are not given a complete picture of that reality. Thus, the day-to-day reality of living with a disability is rarely covered adequately in films. Some which deal more specifically with issues relating to disability or are specifically concerned with disabled people, such as *The Terry Fox Story* (BBC1, 5/7/88), about an amputee who ran across Canada, are able to contain greater detail and cover more issues than those in which the disabled characters are just part of a wider plot. Most of the films portraying disabled characters in major or minor roles contained both positive and negative elements regarding the portrayal of disabled characters. For example, in *23 Paces to Baker Street* (BBC1, 29/7/88) a famous author becomes blind and, as a result, despondent. One night in a pub he overhears some people discussing a crime and goes on to help to solve it. The character is shown as an independent person, not patronised, and respected by those around him. However, in the true Ironside tradition, the blind character is shown to be endowed with Sherlock Holmes-like powers of deduction. The impression created is that, as a result of his lost sight, his perceptiveness and abilities as a detective are greatly enhanced. Again, in the film *Champion* (ITV, 14/9/88), about Bob Champion's fight against cancer and eventual Grand National win, the storyline is a positive one but becomes sentimental in its approach to the triumph of Champion's victory.

The films mentioned to a large extent come from the category of those that dealt with issues relating to disability in some depth. These numbered 25 films, just over $\frac{1}{3}$ of the 72 films in which disability is portrayed and just under $\frac{1}{2}$ of the 53 films featuring major or minor disabled characters. When films as a whole are looked at, a batch of very obvious stereotypes becomes apparent. These broadly fall into three categories: the criminals, the subhumans and the powerless and pathetic characters. Six of the films with major or minor disabled characters showed them as criminals. Four of these were films about murderers portrayed as mentally ill. *Dirty Harry* (BBC1, 19/9/88) is about Scorpio, a killer being pursued by Harry (Clint Eastwood). Throughout the film references are made to the killer's mental instability. *Peeping Tom* (BBC2, 19/11/88) is about a seemingly normal young man who has been driven insane by his father's cruelty, picks up women in order to kill them, and eventually kills himself. *Scream Pretty Peggy* (ITV, 12/7/88) is about a schizophrenic with Mr Hyde-like tendencies, and *When Dreams Come True* (ITV, 9/11/88) revolves around a killer who is said by the police to be mentally ill. The other two films, *Hawk the Slayer* (ITV, 2/9/88) and *Maze* (Channel 4, 9/9/88) have physically disabled villains. In *Hawk the Slayer*, the main villain is particularly nasty, he has no regard for other people's lives and is motivated by the desire for vengeance upon those who scarred his face. This film also portrays a wicked slave trader who mercilessly beats his captives, thinks nothing of burning villages to the ground and kills everyone who gets in his way. Apparently as an embodiment of his evil nature, this character is partially sighted and wears an eyepatch. In each of these films the outcome for the disabled is death.

In all, some 5 films portrayed disabled characters as subhuman or as low life. These were *Blood of the Vampire* (ITV, 17/9/88), *Face at the Window* (Channel 4, 7/10/88), *Born of Fire* (Channel 4, 14/4/88), *Blazing Saddles* (BBC1, 28/5/88) and *Jack the Ripper* (ITV, 11/10/88). In *Jack the Ripper* at one point the police are desperate for some results and so round up some of the down-and-outs from the streets. These turn out to be a bizarre group of characters, mumbling, muttering and yelling, who include two dwarfs. They are mocked and insulted for a while and then given some bread which they all tear at and fight over like a pack of dogs.

Finally, films portraying disabled characters as powerless or pathetic characters numbered 7. These were *Life is a Bed of Roses* (Channel 4, 3/5/88), *Don Juan* (Channel 4, 30/5/88), *Carry on Doctor* (BBC1, 13/8/88), *Trading Places* (ITV, 15/8/88), *The Good, the Bad and the Ugly* (BBC2, 28/8/88), *The Blood Beast Terror* (ITV, 3/9/88) and *Fat Angels* (Channel 4, 28/10/88). Some of these treatments were far more blatant than others, for example, in *Carry on Doctor* Frankie Howerd treated his partially deaf accomplice as a complete idiot, continually raising his eyes skyward and huffing and puffing because she failed to understand or respond to what he said. As we have mentioned, in *The Good, the Bad and the Ugly* a character called 'Half Soldier' gives some information to the character played by Lee Van Cleef. Van Cleef looks on arrogantly, then throws a couple of coins down for the man, who then goes into the saloon shouting for whiskey. As previously mentioned, perhaps 'Half Soldier' is an embodiment of the hardship and violence which the film suggests existed in nineteenth-century America. Perhaps also it is because this character is considered less than fully human that he can pick up information because other people are careless of what they say in his hearing.

Although the dramatic functions of disability were varied and not always clear, it was rare for a disabled person to appear as just another character. In fact in only 9 films were disabled characters portrayed simply as ordinary people without the disability being a major part of the role and in only 4 of these were they major or minor characters. In two of the films, *Gilbert and Sullivan* (Channel 4, 12/5/88) and *The Godfather* (BBC2, 11/9/88), the only reason that disabled people appear is because characters become disabled through age. It is very difficult to identify the precise motives for including disabled characters in background or incidental roles, but there usually seemed to be an ulterior motive for the inclusion. This might be to make more obvious the context of hardship and difficulty or to introduce some other cinematic vignettes about the human condition. In only 5 programmes were they judged as completely neutral. These were two Abbot and Costello films (BBC2, 26/5/88, BBC2, 2/6/88), in which disabled people appeared fleetingly as part of a crowd, *Akenfield* (Channel 4, 2/6/88), in which an old man with two walking sticks is part of a group at a funeral, *Under Fire* (ITV, 24/9/88), in which a man in a wheelchair is seen as one of a group of refugees and *Into the Night* (BBC2, 30/10/88) in which during a crowded airport scene a young woman in a wheelchair is briefly seen.

As we have implied earlier, one possible way of understanding the inclusion of characters with disabilities in films is as a means of suggesting an 'atmosphere' in the film. In some films, particularly those in which disabled characters are cast as criminals, the disability seems to be used as a device to add to the quality of 'menace', or in support of the thoroughgoing alien nature of the criminal character. In *Peeping Tom* (BBC2, 19/11/88) the air of menace is increased by the central character's mental instability and unpredictability. The contradictory possibilities which are introduced by the inclusion of disabled people are illustrated by *Blood of the Vampire* (ITV, 17/9/88), where the mute assistant working for the evil doctor appears to add to the air of menace. Another way of looking at the film is that the doctor is promoting equal employment opportunities for speech-impaired people, but this is evidently not the meaning which we are supposed to extract, although it is difficult to identify precisely the features of the film which encourage us to the former rather than the latter interpretation.

Disability seemed also to be a device used to enhance a desperate, wild and violent atmosphere. For example, in two Westerns, *The Good, The Bad and The Ugly* (BBC2, 28/8/88) and *One-Eyed Jacks* (BBC2, 4/9/88), the West is very wild, violence rules, there are very few comforts or luxuries and the disabled characters reinforce this. The same was true of *Jeremiah Johnson* (ITV, 12/8/88), in which Robert Redford plays a nineteenth-century trapper in the upper reaches of the Rockies. Once again, the few people that live there live 'on the edge', lonely, isolated, hungry and in constant fear of death. At one point in the film this feeling of desperation is emphasised by a woman who appears incoherent, wildly screaming into the wind.

Finally, disability at times appeared to be used to enhance bizarre or mysterious situations. In the film *Clean Slate* (BBC2, 9/9/88) a French policeman is trying to keep law and order in a colonial town. He has problems with some of the colonials and very little control over them. Eventually he takes to shooting them and to framing a disliked colleague. The film is an absurdist black comedy with an air of surrealism about it. Two disabled characters appear in background and incidental roles. One, a native of the area, moves crablike across the scene on two occasions for no apparent reason, and the other, a blind man, is also seen twice in odd circumstances. There is no apparent reason for the inclusion of these two characters, who play no part in the plot and appear only briefly. However, they are both picked out against the general background and made to look odd. This is particularly true of the blind man: we first see him being led through a crowded station by a servant while being jeered at and prodded by a group of youths, and once on the train we see him stumbling through a carriage quoting some poetry to no-one in particular. These two characters emphasised the bizarre nature of the film by the way in which they were portrayed. Similar effects occurred in four other films, two with minor characters, one with a major character and one with background and incidental characters.

CONCLUSION

To sum up, it is difficult to avoid the impression that there is usually an ulterior motive for the inclusion of disabled characters in films and dramas. Perhaps the most obvious is the use of suffering and disadvantage, followed by bravery and willpower, to stir tender emotions in the audience; though as we have noted the mechanisms whereby this occurs remain elusive. Other motives are the use of disabled characters as foils for comedy sketches, or to enhance an atmosphere of deprivation, mystery, violence and menace. A positive role for disabled characters is relatively rare, with most of the characterisations reverting to a stereotype about people with disabilities. This might be the heightening of other senses due to blindness, as in *23 Paces to Baker Street*, or the disability being a physical manifestation of some inner evil, as in *Hawk the Slayer*. But perhaps the most important point to make in summing up is the lack of attention paid to issues that relate to disability, either at a personal level or, more importantly, within society as a whole. This is true of the majority of television output. Perhaps the popular soap operas with their didactic ambitions to deal with important social issues might in the future be able to take a lead in dealing with this problem.

Chapter 5

Comparing the treatment of disabled and able-bodied characters in fictional programmes

Our analysis of dramatic fiction suggests some interesting differences between the ways in which disabled and non-disabled characters are portrayed. In order to explore these differences more systematically, this chapter presents a direct comparison. Earlier (Table 2.6) we reported that of the 4,767 major and minor characters appearing in dramatic fiction in the six week sample period, only 66 (1.4 per cent) were disabled. With such a small number of disabled characters detailed analysis must be limited, and so we shall use as a database for this section the total number of 154 disabled characters appearing both in the main sample and in the supplementary sample of 148 additional programmes.

In comparing the portrayal of disabled people with that of the able-bodied in dramatic fiction a possible source of confusion arises from the fact that some genres of programme are more likely to contain disability than others. From Table 2.2 in Chapter 2 we can calculate that 32 per cent of crime, police and detective programmes showed disability but that only 8 per cent of soap operas did so. Therefore, if comparisons are made between the disabled characters and the subsample of three characters drawn from each dramatic fiction programme this may conflate differences in the way in which disabled and able-bodied characters are portrayed with genre differences. Crime, police and detective programmes show more death and violence, and so the fact that disabled people are more highly represented in this genre might lead to an inflated impression of the numbers of disabled people associated with crime, insanity and death. Therefore, in some instances in the ensuing analysis we will present figures in which this possibility has been controlled for. To do this we take able-bodied characters only from programmes in which disabled people appeared for a comparison. This will be referred to as the restricted sample of characters. We will also compare the treatment and depiction of disabled characters with those of the sample of three able-bodied characters from each programme.

DEMOGRAPHIC COMPARISON OF DISABLED AND ABLE-BODIED CHARACTERS

A convenient starting point for analysis is to examine demographic variables, such as age, sex and social class. By and large there were few noteworthy differences. The overwhelming majority of disabled and able-bodied characters were white (95 per cent in both cases) and mostly male (65 per cent of able-bodied and 71 per cent of disabled characters). Age differences were a little more evident: compared with the able-bodied, disabled characters were more likely to be either under the age of 15 or over the age of 50, as Table 5.1 indicates.

While this chapter does not deal with comparisons between the real world and the world of television, it is worth noting that the age and sex differences between able-bodied and disabled characters are small compared with the considerable differences between the world of television and the UK population in which the age profile of disabled people is skewed toward older age groups.

Table 5.1 Age profiles of disabled and able-bodied populations in dramatic fiction

Age	Disabled		Able-bodied	
	Frequency	Percentage	Frequency	Percentage
80+	4	3	1	0.1
70-79	5	3	7	0.5
60-69	17	11	61	4
50-59	14	9	148	10
40-49	32	21	316	21
30-39	39	25	484	32
20-29	22	14	367	24
16-19	5	3	69	5
0-15	16	10	68	4
Total	154	99	1521	100.6

Note: Not all characters are included in this table as for some the age was difficult to determine

Table 5.2 Professional status of characters in dramatic fiction

Type of occupation	Able-bodied characters Number	Percentage	Disabled characters Number	Percentage
Professional	203	13	7	5
White-collar	109	7	3	2
Blue-collar	140	9	12	8
Unemployed	83	5	19	12
Housewife	54	4	3	2
Care professional	61	4	3	2
Public servant	213	14	8	5
Other/cannot code	672	44	99	64
Total	1535	100	154	100

When the social positions of disabled and able-bodied characters in the television world are compared, it becomes evident that disabled characters are more likely to be lower on the socio-economic scale than their able-bodied counterparts. For example, disabled characters were less likely to be portrayed as professional or white-collar workers; only 6 per cent of them fell into this category, compared with 20 per cent of able-bodied characters. Moreover, 12 per cent of disabled characters, as compared with only 5 per cent of able-bodied characters, were unemployed, as indicated in Table 5.2.

A more general comparison of social status shows that 16 per cent of able-bodied characters were classifiable as being of high status compared to 9 per cent of disabled characters. At the other end of the scale, 9 per cent of disabled characters, as compared with 4 per cent of able-bodied characters, were classified as being of low social status.

ATTITUDES SHOWN TOWARDS DISABLED AND ABLE-BODIED CHARACTERS

As an additional perspective on social status, we also coded the attitudes towards the characters shown by any other character in the programme. While we cannot claim that this list exhausts all the possible attitudes which people might display, it covers some of the more contentious attitudes which are shown towards people with

Table 5.3 Attitudes shown towards characters in dramatic fiction

Attitude	Able-bodied characters		Disabled characters	
	Number	Percentage	Number	Percentage
Sympathy	100	7	53	34
Pity	30	2	19	12
Patronising	219	14	46	30
Sadness	45	3	24	16
Fear	108	7	24	16
Avoidance	47	3	14	9
Attraction	666	43	51	33
Respect	783	51	60	39
Mocking	123	8	16	10
Abuse	200	13	23	15

Note: Percentages add to more than 100 due to more than one attitude being coded for each character

disabilities. Table 5.3 lists the attitudes we examined and the numbers of disabled and able-bodied characters who were in receipt of them.

On some variables such as being the victims of mocking and abuse the able-bodied and people with disabilities were not markedly different. However, disabled people were more regularly objects of sympathy, pity, patronage or sadness than were the able-bodied. They were also over twice as likely to be feared. When divided according to type of disability, nearly 40 per cent of the characters portrayed as being mentally ill were feared, which is consistent with the finding that 43 per cent of mentally ill characters were portrayed as potentially dangerous. Interestingly, people were found to be slightly more likely to show attraction for and respect towards able-bodied characters. Returning to the possibility that these differences may be related to programme genre, let us look at the attitudes shown to the disabled using as our database the restricted sample of characters drawn only from programmes which included at least one disabled character. The results are shown in Table 5.4.

Comparing the percentage figures in Table 5.4 with those in Table 5.3, it is clear that little difference is made by taking only those characters who appeared in programmes where disability was featured. Most notably, able-bodied characters were more likely to be found attractive or worthy of respect by other characters, so that in this set of programmes the contrast is more acute.

Table 5.4 Attitudes shown towards characters in dramatic fiction – in programmes depicting disability

Attitude	Able-bodied characters		Disabled characters	
	Number	Percentage	Number	Percentage
Sympathy	30	9	53	34
Pity	3	1	19	12
Patronising	52	15	46	30
Sadness	12	4	24	16
Fear	34	10	24	16
Avoidance	12	4	14	9
Attraction	183	54	51	33
Respect	220	65	60	39
Mocking	34	10	16	10
Abuse	60	18	23	15

Note: Percentages add to more than 100 due to more than one attitude being coded for each character

RELATIONSHIPS OF CHARACTERS

A further aspect of social position is the kind of relationships that characters are depicted as having with other people. Here, able-bodied and disabled characters were equally likely to have family relationships, with about 40 per cent of each group having some kind of relationship with other family members. Around 50 per cent of all characters had an emotional relationship with someone else. The biggest difference came with sexual relationships, either obvious or implied, where nearly twice as great a proportion of able-bodied as against disabled characters appeared to be involved in sexual relationships, as Table 5.5 indicates.

Table 5.5 Sexual relationships of characters in dramatic fiction

Sexual relationship	Able-bodied characters		Disabled characters	
	Number	Percentage	Number	Percentage
Yes	333	22	18	12
No	1202	78	136	88
Total	1535	100	154	100

More generally, disabled characters were more likely to be 'loners', with 35 per cent of them shown without any associate as against 25 per cent of able-bodied characters. Moreover, in the case of mentally ill characters fewer than half (47 per cent) were portrayed as being part of any group. If we look at the leaders or respected members of groups, then disabled characters were portrayed in these roles in 19 per cent of cases whereas the figure for the able-bodied was 25 per cent.

PERSONALITY, CRIMINALITY AND THE OUTCOMES OF PROGRAMMES

Some stereotyping was evident in the way in which disabled characters were portrayed. This was particularly true of their relationship to crime, where, for example, mentally ill characters were more than three times as likely as able-bodied characters to be portrayed as villains. Seventy per cent of villains in US productions were portrayed as being mentally ill, although only half of the mentally ill characters were of US origin. Mentally ill characters were nearly twice as likely as the able-bodied to be portrayed as evil.

To assess the kinds of personality which characters were depicted as having, they were assessed on a list of personality variables, such as sociability, extroversion, independence, happiness and moodiness, which were coded on a one to five scale. These traits were coded only when they were judged to make up a significant part of a character's personality. For this reason nearly 50 per cent of cases received no such coding.

First, let us consider the disabled characters compared with our full subsample of three non-disabled characters from every dramatic fiction programme. Here, of the cases that received a coding, it was notable that mentally ill characters were over twice as likely as others to be coded as aggressive (15 per cent compared with 6 per cent of the able-bodied characters). Disabled characters were over twice as likely to be portrayed as difficult to get on with (16 per cent of disabled against 7 per cent of able-bodied characters) and 18 per cent of disabled characters were depicted as being 'moody', compared with only 9 per cent of the able-bodied characters. Finally, twice as many disabled as non-disabled characters were portrayed as being sad, introverted or unsociable.

Second, let us compare disabled characters with only those able-bodied characters from our restricted sample who appeared in programmes which portrayed disability. If we express the numbers coded into each category as a proportion of the total number of characters coded on that variable in this restricted sample, then some of the differences already noted are enhanced. For example, disabled characters are now found to be over three times as likely to be portrayed as difficult to get on with (9 per cent able-bodied versus 28 per cent disabled) and nearly three times as likely to be moody (12 per cent able-bodied versus 35 per cent disabled). Disabled people are much more likely than the able-bodied to be depicted as introverted (27 per cent of disabled characters coded on the introversion/extroversion scale, versus 4 per cent of the able-bodied) and the able-bodied were far less likely to be unsociable (5 per cent of the able-bodied versus 19 per cent of disabled characters). Again, twice as many disabled as able-bodied characters were portrayed as sad (19 per cent versus 8 per cent of able-bodied characters).

Overall, these figures suggest that in programmes where disability occurs, the contrasts between the disabled and non-disabled characters are more acute than when we take characters in dramatic fiction as a whole. It should be noted that the percentages with which we are dealing are small; on the variables examined here the majority of characters coded fell at either the positive pole or the midpoint of the scale, and many did not exhibit the trait in so sustained a fashion as to make it susceptible to coding. Even so, this leaves us with considerable grounds for concern about the negative depiction of disabled characters.

Regrettably, we have very little systematic information on the way in which disabled people are treated in society as a whole. What we have is a set of complaints and arguments concerning the behaviours which are most irksome and restricting to people with disabilities. These arguments might be illuminated by some account of the way in which people with disabilities are shown on television. Overall, disabled characters are portrayed in a less favourable light than their able-bodied counterparts. For example, as indicated in Table 5.6, over twice as great a proportion of disabled characters were portrayed as criminals or suspected criminals, compared with our subsample of three characters from all dramatic fiction programmes.

These figures are sustained when we take only those programmes which contain disabled people.

When we look at the threat that characters pose to others, a

Table 5.6 Disabled and able-bodied characters as criminals in dramatic fiction

Type of criminality	Disabled characters		Able-bodied characters	
	Number	Percentage	Number	Percentage
Cannot code	4	2.5	31	2
Definitely criminal	13	8.4	80	5.2
Suggested criminality	12	7.8	57	3.7
Criminally insane	5	3.2	0	0
Not criminal	120	77.9	1367	89.1
Total falling in criminal categories	30	19.4	137	8.9
Total	154	99.8	1535	100

similar pattern is revealed, with 9 per cent of the able-bodied characters being 'sometimes' or 'always' dangerous or threatening to others, compared with 19 per cent of disabled characters. If we look at the restricted sample which includes only those characters who appeared in programmes where disability was depicted, then this difference is eroded slightly, with 13 per cent of non-disabled and 20 per cent of disabled characters being sometimes or always threatening or dangerous to other people.

Mentally ill and mentally handicapped characters come off particularly badly in these terms, with nearly half (39 per cent) depicted as being criminally inclined. Of the mentally ill, 44 per cent were depicted as being sometimes or always dangerous to others, and they were more likely to be aggressors, with over one-third of them being so, compared with 16 per cent of disabled characters in general and 12 per cent of able-bodied characters overall. Disabled characters were over twice as likely as the able-bodied to be victims of violence, with 21 per cent of disabled characters and 10 per cent of able-bodied characters falling victim to other characters' violent tendencies.

We should note that the representation of people with disabilities as criminals was one of the key reasons for the development of the character of Nina in *Crossroads*. In the early 1980s, one of the ITV companies showed a film which featured a disabled person as a murderer. This so incensed members of organisations which represented people with disabilities that they began negotiations with the company to 'undo' the damage done. This was the beginning of the idea for the inclusion of Nina in *Crossroads*. (See below, pp. 124 and 132.) To their credit, the television company accepted the criticisms and agreed to develop the character as requested. They also agreed never to re-show the film in question. It should be noted that this was not the first time that *Crossroads* had featured a disabled character. Meg Richardson's son, Sandy, who was confined to a wheelchair as the result of a car accident, featured in the soap throughout the 1970s.

A difference in the treatment of characters regarding their eventual fate was also evident. Disabled characters were over three times as likely as able-bodied characters to be dead by the end of the programme. Overall, 16 per cent of disabled characters did not survive to the end of the programme. Over 50 per cent of these fatalities were violent. Of the violent deaths, over half were caused by the forces of good, mainly the police. A fifth of the violent deaths were suicides, all committed by mentally ill characters. The remaining violent deaths were murders. The non-violent deaths of the disabled characters were regularly depicted as being a result of their disabilities. Nearly half of the non-violent deaths were of this type, forming 22 per cent of all deaths of disabled people. The remaining non-violent deaths occurred as a result of old age or natural causes.

If we take the restricted sample of able-bodied people from programmes in which people with disabilities appeared, then the greater likelihood of death for disabled people is sustained, with 11 per cent of able-bodied and 21 per cent of disabled characters dying.

There is a notable tradition in entertainment and literature of using disabled people to shock or scare the audience or other characters, in the manner of Mr Hyde, Frankenstein's Monster or the Phantom of the Opera. Even though only 4 disabled characters were included in the horror genre, 27 per cent of disabled characters seemed to be used to shock or scare to some extent. The context of such portrayals varies a great deal, however, with a large proportion of mentally ill characters (63 per cent) falling into this category. These characters tended to be disturbed criminals, for example, in the film *Peeping Tom* (BBC2, 19/11/88), which concerned a young man whose problems stemmed from his mistreatment as a child and who murdered young women while filming them. However, not all instances of characters being used to scare involved criminality. For example, Nick in *The Deer Hunter* (BBC2, 2/10/88) ends up playing Russian roulette for money in a club in Saigon and thus kills himself. Judging by the needle marks on his arms, he is also depicted as an intravenous drug-user. In this case mental instability is not used directly to scare, but seems to be used to shock, as an incisive way of signifying how this man's war experiences have eroded his personality and integrity. Like Mr Hyde, mental problems and even physical changes are presented as the result of a disintegration of the will or an erosion of the self.

Drama programmes seem seldom to be used to create more awareness of disability and the problems faced by people with disabilities. The physical problems of being disabled were dealt with in any depth in only 16 per cent of the cases analysed. Usually, mobility difficulties, access to buildings and other problems were ignored. Furthermore, it was unlikely, when disabled characters appeared, that any issues would be raised concerning other people's attitudes to the disabled or society's failure to recognise their special needs; in 75 per cent of cases there was no mention of such issues.

As we might expect from the evidence so far, it was rare for disabled characters to speak out against inequality or discrimination. Of the 154 disabled character appearances, only 24 per cent made any sort of complaint about the way in which they were treated, and these complaints were likely to be directed against individuals and not against general social attitudes and values. In all cases these complaints were put forward by individuals and were not presented as consistent, politicised arguments emerging from groups of people. The only mention of an organised stance against discrimination occurred in *Coming Home* (22/7/88), in which a character played by Jane Fonda attempts to persuade a group of disabled Vietnam war veterans to stand up for their rights as a group, although in the end they decide not to do this.

CONCLUSION AND CONSTRAINTS ON INTERPRETATION

Although this chapter has not covered every aspect of the stereotypical treatment of disabled characters, it has provided quantitative evidence that negative stereotyping exists in television, whereby disabled characters are depicted negatively more often than are their able-bodied counterparts. Whether we take dramatic fiction as a whole, or only those programmes where disability appears, the negative depiction of disabled people is sustained.

It is important to note that our analysis does not exhaust the issue of stereotyping. We have not studied the nuances of particular depictions of able-bodied versus disabled people. We have taken a rather crude notion of stereotyping by comparing disabled and able-bodied characters in relation to certain variables. Arguably, this does not entirely capture the construct of a stereotype, which should also take account of the peculiarities and idiosyncrasies attributed to the stereotyped group. Moreover, we have compared disabled people with 'normal' characters, rather than, for example, with stereotypes of excellence, which may play a large part in the portrayal of leading characters and heroes.

The strength of our work, however, is that it provides an overall account of the position of disabled people on British peak time television. We would argue that it is representative and has achieved a high degree of fidelity to the complex television world it seeks to describe. Therefore we conclude that the stereotyping described here is representative of recent television output and should be of concern both to broadcasters and to those who campaign on disability issues.

Chapter 6

The representation of disability in UK and US drama

In the final chapter of this part of our report we will compare and contrast the way in which characters with disabilities were presented in UK- and US-produced dramatic fiction. In doing this we shall use the sample of 154 programmes taken from both the official six week sample and the supplementary sample of programmes considered to be of particular interest to the project.

We will look at a number of demographic features of this sample, namely, the sex ratio, the age distribution, the ethnic origin and the socio-economic status of disabled and non-disabled characters. Also we will look at the relationships in which the characters were involved and whether they were married; the kinds of personality traits which they exhibited; and the attitudes which other people showed towards them.

The purpose of comparing UK and US programmes is not to determine whether there are any differences between British and American programmes, since the programmes from the US are quite possibly not representative of all US programmes; rather, it is to assess the contribution which US programmes make to the representation of disabled people on British TV.

DEMOGRAPHIC FEATURES

Sex differences

A total of 75 disabled characters appeared in major or minor roles in US productions. Of these, 19 (25 per cent) were female. Of the 64 disabled characters appearing in UK productions 18 (28 per cent) were female. There was thus little difference in the proportions of female disabled characters in UK and US productions, with both countries showing a disproportionately small number.

Age differences

Using our subsample of three characters from each drama programme we can compare the age profiles of disabled and non-disabled characters in UK and US drama. Table 6.1 gives the age distribution of the characters sampled.

When US productions contained disabled people they were more likely than UK productions to include younger disabled people in the storyline. Thirty-one (41 per cent) of the 75 disabled characters in US productions were coded as under 30, compared with 11 (17 per cent) of the disabled characters in UK programmes in this age group. In both countries' productions the majority of the disabled people were aged between 30 and 49. Thirty-five (47 per cent) of the US disabled characters were in this category compared with 34 (53 per cent) of the disabled characters in UK productions. UK productions portrayed more disabled characters aged over 60 than did US productions, with 10 (16 per cent) of the UK disabled characters being coded as over 60 compared to only 4 (5 per cent) in US productions. The majority of able-bodied characters coded were between the ages of 30 and 49 for both countries, with 56 per cent of the US's and 49 per cent of the UK's able-bodied characters appearing in this group.

Ethnic origin

In US productions 96 per cent of all characters were white, 4 per cent black and there were no Asian or Oriental characters. In UK productions almost 97 per cent of characters were white, 3 per cent were black and only 0.43 per cent were Asian or Oriental. According to the OPCS survey (Martin, Meltzer and Eliot, 1988) there is little difference between the rates of incidence of disability between ethnic groups once their different age profiles have been corrected for. However, none of the 64 disabled characters appearing in UK productions were drawn from ethnic minority groups. Of the 38 black characters appearing in US productions, 3 (8 per cent) were disabled. This suggests multiple discrimination against members of minority groups.

Table 6.1 Differences in age grouping in UK and US dramatic fiction

	Country							
	UK				US			
	Able-bodied		Disabled		Able-bodied		Disabled	
Age group	Number	Percentage	Number	Percentage	Number	Percentage	Number	Percentage
0-15	36	4	2	3	21	4	12	16
16-19	38	5	2	3	22	4	1	1
20-29	221	26	7	11	106	20	18	24
30-39	238	28	17	27	204	38	25	33
40-49	179	21	17	27	97	18	10	13
50-59	81	10	7	11	49	9	5	7
60-69	40	5	6	9	22	4	4	5
70-79	4	0.5	3	5	6	1	0	0
80+	0	0	1	2	1	0.2	0	0
Cannot code	4	0.5	2	3	7	1	0	0
Total	841	100	64	101	535	99.2	75	99

Socio-economic status

In both US and UK productions the disabled characters were far less likely to be portrayed as professional people, with similarly small proportions being depicted, as illustrated in Table 6.2. In UK productions able-bodied and disabled characters were about equally likely to be shown as unemployed, but in US productions disabled characters were far more likely to be unemployed (15 per cent appeared to be) than were able-bodied characters. The unemployed constituted the largest single group of US disabled characters, apart from the 'other' category which contained a variety of different occupations including being retired.

The public service category in Table 6.2 includes, for example, teachers and the police. In US productions 23 per cent of able-bodied characters were coded as being in public service, but no disabled characters were coded into this category, compared with 12 per cent of disabled characters in UK productions.

The 'other' category was composed mainly of people who were retired. There was a larger percentage of UK disabled characters than US disabled characters so classified. This difference may be explained by the fact that the disabled people in the US productions in our sample were more likely to come from younger age groups than those in UK productions and would thus be less likely to be over retiring age.

Both countries had a similarly high proportion of disabled

Table 6.2 Occupations of disabled and able-bodied characters in UK and US dramatic fiction

| | Country | | | |
| | UK | | US | |
	Able-bodied Percentage	Disabled Percentage	Able-bodied Percentage	Disabled Percentage
Professional	15	3	16	5
White-collar	11	2	4	1
Blue-collar	14	6	4	9
Unemployed	7	8	3	15
Housewife	4	0	3	3
Care professional	3	0	6	4
Public service	13	12	23	0
Other	31	47	40	35
Cannot code	2	22	1	29
Total	100	100	100	101

characters in the 'cannot code' category (US 29 per cent, UK 22 per cent) compared with able-bodied characters whose occupations were more readily coded, with only 1 per cent of US and 2 per cent of UK able-bodied characters being uncodable. Perhaps this difference is due to the fact that the disabled characters were not always presented in an occupational context, or it may relate to the relative lack of depth in characterisation of disabled people in television drama.

PERSONALITY CHARACTERISTICS IN UK VERSUS US DRAMA PRODUCTIONS

Overall, disabled characters in US drama were more likely to be coded as having more positive personality characteristics than were disabled characters in UK drama, as indicated in Table 6.3.

Table 6.3 shows that US disabled characters were more likely to be shown as being sociable, extrovert, moral and non-aggressive than were UK disabled characters. Conversely, UK disabled characters were more often shown as dependent, sad, moody and difficult than disabled characters in US productions.

As well as their own personality traits, the attitudes which other characters showed towards disabled characters were also coded, to throw light on the social milieu in which disabled people were represented.

Table 6.3 Differences in personality traits between characters in UK and US productions

	Country	
	UK	US
Personality trait	Percentage	Percentage
Sociable	30	53
Extrovert	30	41
Liked	36	59
Moral	14	28
Non-aggressive	19	36
Dependent	55	19
Sad	27	11
Moody	44	11
Difficult	36	9

Note: Columns add to more than 100 due to more than one category being coded for each character appearance

Table 6.4 Attitudes shown towards disabled characters in UK and US productions

Attitude shown	Country	
	UK Percentage	US Percentage
Treated like any other person	57	71
Attraction	30	34
Fear	15	17
Abuse	19	6
Pity	16	7
Mockery	13	6
Avoidance	10	7
Respect	25	46
Patronage	40	18
Aggression	9	20
None of the above	10	17

Note: Columns add to more than 100 due to more than one category being coded for each character appearance

ATTITUDES SHOWN TOWARDS DISABLED CHARACTERS

Generally, more positive attitudes were shown towards disabled people in US programmes than towards disabled people in UK productions, as indicated in Table 6.4.

Disabled characters in US productions were more likely to be treated like any other person or with respect, and were less likely to be abused, pitied, mocked or patronised than were disabled characters in UK productions. Given the higher profile adopted by disabled people in US society, this is perhaps not surprising. However, aggression was more likely to be shown towards disabled characters in US productions, although this may be due to the fact that the US programmes shown in this country are in general more violent than UK productions.

RELATIONSHIPS OF CHARACTERS IN UK AND US DRAMATIC FICTION

The kinds of relationships which disabled people are depicted in

It has been suggested that one of the problems encountered by disabled people is that of forming relationships with others: that is,

Table 6.5 Percentage of able-bodied and disabled people involved in different types of relationship in UK and US television productions

Relationship type	Country			
	UK		US	
	Able-bodied	Disabled	Able-bodied	Disabled
Emotional	42	26	47	63
Sexual	19	8	23	11
Family	44	31	36	36
Potential relationship	22	9	20	5
No relationships	10	12	10	23
Total	137	86	136	138

Note: Percentages add to more or less than 100 due to more than one category being coded in some cases and no category being coded in others

other people may not to wish to have them as friends or workmates or lovers. To investigate whether this discrimination is apparent from the television portrayal of disability, and whether it differs between the US and the UK, the kinds of relationships in which disabled people were depicted were coded and compared with the sorts of relationships that the able-bodied were shown to have. The results are shown in Table 6.5.

Disabled characters appearing in US productions were more likely than any other group to be coded as having an emotional relationship (63 per cent). By contrast, UK disabled characters were far less likely to have an emotional relationship (26 per cent). In both US and UK productions disabled characters were less likely to be portrayed as having a sexual relationship (8 per cent in UK, 11 per cent in US), compared to able-bodied characters (23 per cent in US, 19 per cent in UK). In US productions disabled and able-bodied characters were equally likely to have family relationships (36 per cent). In UK productions, however, disabled characters were less likely than able-bodied characters to be portrayed as part of a family (31 per cent of disabled characters and 44 per cent of the able- bodied).

Disabled characters in both US and UK productions were far less likely to be coded as having a potential relationship (5 per cent in the US and 9 per cent in the UK) than were able-bodied characters (20 per cent in the US and 22 per cent in the UK). In both US and UK productions 10 per cent of the able-bodied characters were portrayed as having no relationships. The UK disabled characters were only slightly higher at 12 per cent, but the US disabled characters were more than twice as likely to have no relationships (23 per cent). In both countries the majority of these were physically disabled (UK 56 per cent, US 53 per cent).

COMPARING UK AND US DRAMATIC FICTION BY GENRE

A table indicating the different genres of programme that we are concerned with was presented in Chapter 2 (Table 2.2). In order to make comparisons between the UK and the US we have combined some of the genres listed there, since some of them had very few disabled people in them. In this section we propose to deal with the following groups of programme genres:

i)   Crime, thriller, spy programmes
ii)   Historical drama and other drama
iii) Soap operas
iv)   Situation comedies
v)   Children's productions

Let us take these in order.

Crime, thriller and spy programmes

During the sampling period an equal number of US and UK programmes were coded in this genre, with 27 for each country, making a total of 57. More US productions contained more examples of disability: 37 per cent as against 26 per cent of UK productions.

Table 6.6   Numbers of crime, thriller and spy programmes featuring disability

| | Country | | |
	UK	US	Total
Crime, thriller and spy	7	10	17

When comparisons are made with other dramatic genres, the proportion of characters with a disability shown in crime, thriller and spy programmes is notably high. This does not imply that makers of crime, thriller and spy programmes are more concerned to include disabled people in their productions. It may be that the connection perceived between disability and crime, noted in Chapter 5, results in the relatively higher number of disabled people appearing in programmes of this type.

Historical drama and other drama

Sixty-four (57 per cent) of the programmes in this category coded in our sample were made in the UK, compared with 45 (39 per cent) which were of US origin, giving a total of 115. More US productions contained characters with a disability than did UK productions, with 42 per cent of US and 19 per cent of UK productions including such characters.

The differences in the proportions of programmes featuring disability might be connected with the kind of drama productions from each country. Many of the UK productions containing characters with a disability were either film or single drama productions, for example *Family Life* (BBC1, 3/6/88). By comparison, the characters with disabilities shown in US productions tended to appear in serials, for example, *LA Law* (ITV, 12/5/88, 19/5/88 and 2/6/88), which accounted for 3 of the total of 154 disabled character appearances coded during the study.

Table 6.7   Numbers of historical and other drama programmes featuring disability

	Country		
	UK	US	Total
Historical and other drama	12	19	31

Soap operas

Thirteen (13 per cent) of the soap opera episodes coded in the six week sampling period were of US origin. None of these portrayed disability. This could be linked to the contention that US drama of this kind is not 'realistic' and that, for example, *Dallas* and *Dynasty* are sufficiently detached from everyday reality to avoid featuring any disability at all. This argument raises questions about what we mean by realism. In what sense is *Eastenders* more realistic than *Dallas*? Is it to do with geographical and cultural proximity? It is unlikely that many who consider *Eastenders* realistic actually know people like those portrayed in it, and yet the characters depicted are somehow believable. We do not have the space here to probe this issue further. Fifty-nine (60 per cent) of the soap operas coded were UK productions. Only 2 of these portrayed disabled characters, with *Brookside* (Channel 4, 17/5/88) the only one to feature a permanently disabled character, 'Sizzler', a villain with a stammer.

Situation comedies

Situation comedies accounted for almost a quarter (22 per cent) of the total number of drama programmes coded during the sampling period. Sixty-one (65 per cent) of these were UK productions of which 6 (10 per cent) featured disabled characters. By comparison, out of the 32 US situation comedies, 2 (6 per cent) featured someone with a disability. Thus there were 92 situation comedies in all, of which 8 contained a person with some disability.

Children's productions

During the sampling period 29 children's programmes of UK origin were coded compared with 9 US productions. Of the 29 UK children's programmes, 2 (7 per cent) featured someone with a disability. Only one of the 9 US programmes did so.

CONCLUSION

It is tempting to conclude this section by making some overall comments about the depiction of disability in UK and US drama. However, as already noted, this could be misleading since the US programmes broadcast in the UK may not be representative of US television output as a whole. One might attempt to relate the different depictions in UK and US productions to the values which we may believe to be current in the two societies; we might relate the somewhat more positive depiction of disabled people in US drama, especially in respect of their personality traits and the attitudes shown to them by other people, to the greater prominence given to the rights of the disabled in US society. This also must be avoided due to the possibly unrepresentative nature of the US sample.

If we find the relatively less favourable position of disabled people in UK as against US programmes (in our sample) distasteful, then we must pause to consider the relation that we wish television to have to reality. Many disabled people can attest to the often shabby treatment that they receive at the hands of able-bodied society. Should television be blamed for depicting or reflecting this? The issue becomes more complex still when we consider the difficulty of discerning whether the context of the unpleasant treatment shows that it is improper. We could argue that as part of its public service role television should show more positive images of disabled people, and that US and UK television could learn something from each other. A similar argument about the depiction of disability could be advanced to one which is used in relation to women and black people. If women are underrepresented in high status jobs in our society, is this sufficient excuse for television not to show them as executives, doctors and politicians? Perhaps television has a duty to show a less discriminatory world than the one which exists outside, in the hope that this may encourage the exterior reality to become less harsh for those who are the victims of discrimination.

Part II

The portrayal of people with disabilities on television: a commentary

Part II

The portrayal of people
with disabilities on
television: a commentary

Chapter 7

Introduction
Definitions and stereotypes

It is often argued that television ought to deal with the 'experience of disability': what Alan Sutherland has termed

> the ... question of getting on and living our own lives in the face of widespread discrimination and failure to cater for our own needs.
> (Sutherland, 1981, p. 22)

That is a legitimate demand since – as our data show – that experience is not commonly seen on television. But it is a demand made of a medium which is essentially two-dimensional and which favours stereotypical images, and eschews the full richness of characters and cultures. In other words, it rarely deals with issues sensitively, particularly those issues which are now of increasing concern to many: sexism, racism, 'age-ism' and, one should now add, the treatment of people with disabilities (what in the US is now called 'handicappism'). As one television producer remarked:

> The clarification of the stereotype [on television] is never made ... the disability problem is part of the broader arena of 'care' that needs enormous pressure to change.

It is the medium's inability to deal with issues and concepts 'in depth' which inevitably leads to criticism. Whether it is industrial relations news or the treatment of ethnic groups or gay people, the problems are not dissimilar: namely, television works with conventions – the stereotype, the sitcom, the quiz programme, the one-off play – which package shallow characterisations for the purpose of holding the viewers' attention. It is rarely used to create understanding and to question common assumptions.

Those who criticise television as currently experienced believe that it fails to portray 'accurately' certain sections of society so that those who depend on television for information about the outside world obtain a 'distorted' view of its workings and constituent parts. Thus, in the context of the present study one could argue that the way in which television portrays people with disabilities fails to touch upon their 'ordinariness' and humanity as well as upon society's role in discriminating against people with disabilities. By employing certain stereotypes, for example, the courageous disabled person facing up to adversity, it does not give an adequate account of the everyday experience of the majority of people with disabilities and of those close to them who, like the able-bodied more generally, stumble from day to day. Rather, it plays upon the courage and determination of the individual in question who appears as a shining example to the rest of us. People with disabilities, as well as the able-bodied, are then supposed to admire and emulate the courageous few; our own everyday problems then appear petty in comparison with the superhuman efforts which the documentaries often focus on. On what grounds can we complain and moan about our own, by comparison, minor problems?

Another consequence of the use of stereotypes and particularly the use of individuals (whether courageous or otherwise) is that it individualises the 'problem' rather than universalising it and examining society's share of the blame. Thus,

the bravery stereotype is obviously an attractive one but it supports our oppression very strongly, by making disability a purely individual responsibility.

(Quoted in O'Neill, 1988, p. 23)

It then becomes possible to lose sight of the overall nature of the issue.

Many believe that the almost total exclusion of characters with disabilities from soaps accentuates the problem in that the one format in which everyday 'ordinariness' is most visible and accessible lacks wholeness. Instead of a 'slice of human life' which would necessarily include people with disabilities, one sees only a dramatised fragment of human life. As one respondent put it:

In major soaps, it [an appearance of a disabled character] just doesn't happen. You don't see children with special needs for example. It's just normal, happy, bubbly life that you see.

All these points will be examined at greater length below, but there is one final consideration which must be mentioned here. Television, as it enters the era of deregulation, may increasingly turn to what is inexpensive and, in addition, least troublesome. As these pressures are felt within the medium it may indeed be the whole area of 'care' that is abandoned or sent to the fringes of the production system. These pressures are not new, but it is worth noting that all the producers interviewed expressed a degree of concern about the direction in which television reforms are driving the medium and the consequences of such reforms.

These general points should not be seen as an apology for television's shortcomings; nor are they an explanation of them. They do, however, provide a backdrop to understanding the complex process of programme production in a medium that is faced by numerous pressures from a variety of quarters.

In this part of the study we attempt to establish what are the main factors which account for the ways in which people with disabilities are portrayed on television. It is based on a series of interviews with television producers and writers and on group discussions. Fuller details of these can be found in Appendix III.

Neither the group discussions nor the interviews with television workers were the results of 'statistical sampling' methods. In both cases, a variety of contacts and leads took the researcher into different areas; one interview could generate the names of others deemed worth talking to or would provide the setting for a group discussion. Nevertheless, an attempt was made to canvass a wide range of views. Inevitably, someone or something important was missed; television, even with only four channels, generates a minimum of about 80 hours per day and no partial monitoring can be fully representative.

This chapter discusses general issues concerning the portrayal of people with disabilities on television. Throughout the report reference will be made to a survey of public attitudes to disability and its portrayal on television, which was conducted by the BBC on behalf of the Broadcasting Research Unit. This will be discussed more fully in Chapter 8. Details of the questions asked are included in Appendix IV. Chapter 9 deals with the supply of actors with disabilities and the specific problems of casting actors with disabilities in television programmes. Finally, Chapter 10 concerns the central questions of why television portrays people with disabilities in particular ways and the particular pressures that producers and writers work under. These chapters are based mainly on the interviews and group discussions.

THE PORTRAYAL OF PEOPLE WITH DISABILITIES ON TELEVISION

Our analysis of the portrayal of people with disabilities confirms a widely accepted view that representations of such people on the television or cinema screens emphasise certain types of character-isations and certain stereotypes. In a recent account of such images, Longmore (1987, pp. 65–79) listed some of the representations. These included:

- disability or physical handicaps as an emblem of evil
- the disabled as 'monsters'
- disability as a loss of one's humanity
- disability as total dependency and a lack of self-determination
- the image of the disabled as a maladjusted person
- disability as compensation or the idea of the substitute gift (for example, the blind having 'other' [unnamed] gifts)
- disability leading to courageousness or achievement
- disability and sexuality: as sexual menace, deviancy, danger stemming from the loss of control (for example, Dr Strangelove)

Others could be added:

- disability as an object of fun or pity
- the disabled as the object of charity

What is missing from these portrayals – and one must remember that according to Longmore there are 'hundreds of characters with all sorts of disabilities on our screens' – is the portrayal of people with disabilities as an integral part of life: that is, television does not portray people with disabilities as part of everyday modern life. When people with disabilities do appear on the screen, their presence and their actions are determined by the nature of their disabilities. Thus, a person with a disability might appear as an object of pity (or charity), as an object of wonder (to encourage us all) or as a tragic figure (because of the disability); he/she is much less likely to appear as a person, an individual, who happens also to have a disability. This is a crucial point, and it is one that was repeatedly made by members of the discussion groups. People, and television, saw the disability rather than the person; or, put another way, they saw the person through the disability.

Keeping people with disabilities away from the more popular programme genres exacerbates the issue, since it further isolates them from the mainstream of life (from which they are already largely excluded). As members of discussion groups often asked: where were the disabled people in soap operas? Why were they absent from advertisements? Where were they in quiz programmes? If they are commonly seen in our society, why are they absent from those media which supposedly reflect that society? Why must they be segregated from the mainstream and disenfranchised? Why are they so often shown as housebound individuals unable to cope with life and dependent on others?

As one respondent put it:

> You walk down the streets and you see blacks who are easily visible; there are gays, they are not easily visible; and there are people with disabilities. You see them everywhere. This isn't reflected on television.... People with disabilities ought to be as much part of television as they are part of, or should be part of, society.
>
> (Quoted in O'Neill, 1988, p. 7)[1]

Television's overconcentration on a disability per se to the exclusion of the individual concerned and his/her humanity was the source of many critical comments. As one young woman with a disability remarked: 'my disability does not worry me but it worries other people'. A similar comment was made by a respondent who was totally blind: 'the fact that I am blind does not take up much of my time; it does not overwhelm my thoughts. My time is taken up coping with my life'. Or, 'because we have a disability, it does not mean we haven't got a brain'.

These remarks reflect a now widely held view about the deficiencies of all media in their coverage of people with disabilities. This view was articulated by the American Department of Rehabilitation when it published its guidelines for eliminating 'stereotypes and handicappism'. Some of its many questions are very pertinent. It asked:

> Do images convey the abilities and power and 'accentuate the positive' of characters with disabling conditions, or is disability the

sum total or most important part of the person? Are disabling conditions or labels used to evoke ridicule? Do images stimulate pity, distance, charity or feelings of superiority over the person with a disability?

(Scott-Parker, 1989, pp. 15–16)

According to the Department of Rehabilitation:

'Handicappism' debases like racism or sexism. 'Handicappism' is a cultural and social set of practices and attitudes which defines people as burdens, less than human or deserving or able to maintain and contribute to [society]. Stereotyped images ... define people by their disability ... people with differences (should be) seen first and foremost as people.

(Scott-Parker, 1989, p. 16)

It is important that this situation is thoroughly examined since it is central to most critiques of the media in this area. Because television, and one must say the public at large, understands disability as a purely physical phenomenon – a physical limitation – it cannot explore the other dimension of the issue, namely, disability as socially constructed. Equally important, it cannot grasp the degree of independence which many people wish for. The physical difference gets in the way of proper understanding and becomes an issue in itself; the physical difference becomes the point of ridicule, the source of pity, the mark of difference.

Precisely the same problem arises in the context of statistical studies which attempt to quantify 'the prevalence of disability' in society. Thus, although the OPCS has made efforts to avoid a mechanistic and static description of disability, its many critics allege that it has failed because it takes account of only the physical traits of disability. It classifies what people with disabilities cannot physically do or cope with. It does not identify a person with a disability but a disabled person. It thus cannot respond to the ways in which society's attitudes and structures restrict the potential of people with disabilities.

According to some of its critics, despite its sophistication, the OPCS has remained wedded to a 'medical model' of disability

which sees disability in terms of personal tragedy, a 'burden' belonging to the individual whose bodily condition prevents the person from playing an active and equal part in society. This medical condition is fixed and can be changed only by medical intervention – i.e. 'cured'.

(GMCDP, 1988, p. 4)

Many people with disabilities, and others, have found this model unsatisfactory and have preferred to use the 'social model' in which

the roots of the 'difficulties' faced by disabled people ... [arise] from a society dominated by able-bodied people who consciously or otherwise 'marginalise disabled people'.

(GMCDP, 1984, p. 4)

From this latter perspective, it is society which 'stigmatises' and discriminates against people with disabilities.

Such a reappraisal of the meaning of disability must affect efforts to classify people with disabilities. If 'the meaning of disability' derives largely from its social context, then categories which are based on medical traits alone cannot touch upon the real meaning of disability, for example discrimination, and they are bound to be inadequate.

To quote Allan Sutherland:

Ultimately, any definition which separates people into 'disabled' and 'able-bodied' is on one level extremely unsatisfactory, because it perpetuates what one might refer to as the 'myth of the normal healthy body' ... but very few people have bodies that work with 100 per cent efficiency.

(Sutherland, 1981, p. 17)

He goes on to argue:

The true picture of disablement as a range of disorders of varying severity, each one covering a diversity of individual cases, is lost, and those 'below the line' are stigmatised.

(p. 18)

Society thus discriminates against people with disabilities in such a way as to deny people 'the means to exercise their capabilities' (p. 22); or as others have defined it, disability is

the disadvantage of restriction of activity caused by contemporary social organisations which take little or no account of people who are physically impaired (lacking part of a limb or having a defective organ, limb or mechanism of the body) and thus excludes them from participation in the mainstream of social activities ... disability is therefore a particular form of social oppression.

(GMCDP, 1988, p. 5)

The importance of this critique of the medical model is that it not only blurs the easy categorisations which the public usually associates with disability but also challenges those who perceive disablement as a condition to be pitied because it is a condition regarded as 'somehow less than human' (Longmore, 1987, p. 68). The reality is quite the opposite: for some the experience of discrimination and even oppression leads to the development of a 'disability culture' which rejoices in and feeds on the meaning of difference.

Although this is not the place for an analysis and critique of these various positions, it must be pointed out that the developing conception of disability as a social condition lies at the heart of contemporary attempts to improve the situation. Whether in the arts or in the world of television, at work or in sport, the social model has nourished and lent support to those who believe that they have been discriminated against for too long. They no longer want to be outside society, segregated from many of its aspects; they want to be integrated within it. For this group, this would have the added advantage of familiarising the able-bodied with people with disabilities.

The point is not that people with disabilities want to deny the physical nature of their conditions. They want to emphasise that those differences do not, and should not, deny their existence as individuals in the eyes of the able-bodied. As one discussant put it:

As a disabled person you are either ignored or taken over [by the able-bodied]. You have to prove that you are capable of doing things in a way that others do not.

Discussants resorted to a number of examples to illustrate the 'social model' described above. One way is to follow through the criticisms that highlight society's inadequate provision of facilities, for example, access, which would enable people with disabilities to play a full part within it. But more important and perhaps more fruitful is the exploration of some of the (public) attitudes which 'disable' people. One particularly powerful example was provided by a man who was totally blind:

One finds many examples of attitudes in society which disable you. For example, as a disabled person I had been visited by a Superintendent of the Police a number of years ago and initially requested not to take my children out on the street on my own. His officers were fed up with getting telephone calls about this blind fellow wandering about with a baby in his arms and a toddler at his side.

Another example is directly related to the theme of this research and it comes from a documentary made for BBC's *Forty Minutes*. The programme featured a woman, Alison French, who had cerebral palsy. In that programme, Alison is shown shopping with her (able-bodied) husband in a supermarket and at some point during that scene she kisses her husband. For her, this act is a defiance of convention and public expectations, a political act. Rarely do we see such acts in public or on the screen, and when we do see them the reaction is one of surprise or even shock. Yet, and this was the point of the example, it is our expectations and also television's which need to be examined; so rarely are the disabled seen doing what others do as a matter of course that the reaction is one of surprise and bewilderment.

The theme of discrimination and stigma was also raised by discussants in answer to questions about their own ideas of the meaning of disability. Thus:

Anything that so-called 'normal' people fail to accept.

(An able-bodied carer)

Social oppression.

(An able-bodied carer)

Generally people categorise you and don't give you your own identity.

(A person with a disability)

People overlook you and don't talk to you straight. They talk across you. It's the 'does he take sugar?' sort of attitude. They ignore you.

(A person with a disability)

It would be an exaggeration to suggest that all members of the discussion groups shared these views of 'the meaning of disability'. Some individuals and some groups were more sensitive and aware than others and some (able-bodied) professional carers had a more clearly defined perspective than others. In some groups, the 'social oppression' perspective, for instance, was accepted as a valid and accurate description of the situation. When the term 'social oppression' was used in another setting, it met with bemused looks. The essence of what was intended was not doubted, but the terminology – borrowed from other social and political struggles – appeared too heavy-handed. Nevertheless, throughout the discussions with people with disabilities and professional or voluntary carers, numerous examples were given to highlight the extent to which people with disabilities 'suffer' or are excluded from the 'normal' social, leisure and economic processes of life.

This was particularly evident in one discussion group which was made up of parents and carers. The views of disability expressed focused on the idea of 'range' rather than the easy categorisation of people with disability. However, there was a division of opinion as to how to classify types of disability such as epilepsy and diabetes. To one member of the group, what mattered was the extent 'to which medical treatment allowed the individual to lead a normal life'. Thus, if the diabetic was able to control his/her condition and lead a 'normal' life, he/she could not be said to be disabled. Admittedly, such an individual would have to make an extra effort to cope with life but this was not, according to this respondent, any different from most members of society.

Despite this difference of opinion over the nature of disability and whether one had to take into account the fact that, in some cases, some disabilities are not permanent conditions, which would affect any definition offered, all members of the group were able to offer examples of the ways in which societal processes limit the lives of those with a disability. In other words, although the social model was not fully articulated, all were able to illustrate the ways in which society 'disables' people with disabilities. It was not then simply a matter of a once and for all medical condition which determined one's life; the provision of facilities and the nature of the environment were critical to understanding the meaning of disability. We return to this when we analyse the data on public attitudes in Chapter 8.

The people with disabilities who were interviewed for this project were, by and large, also able to support their views by citing examples of the ways in which society restricts their lives. What they wanted people to understand and the media to represent was their 'ordinariness' and 'humanity' and not their differences; differences which, as noted above, only complicate their lives rather than put them apart from others in society. In other words, they want to move away from being portrayed as 'people coping wonderfully with life despite their differences' and to be seen as living their own lives on their own terms.

And to live one's own life on one's own terms means, in effect, to reject society's attitudes about disabilities and television's portrayals which emphasise dependency and debilitating differences. The 'I didn't know they could do that' sort of public reaction is itself evidence of widespread ignorance and a lack of understanding of the lives of those who have disabilities. Paradoxically, the way to alter these attitudes and perceptions may not lie with television programmes which feature people with disabilities sailing, swimming, taking part in the Paralympics and so forth, since such programmes reinforce the separateness which people with disabilities wish to overcome. Quite simply, if people with disabilities are part of our society they ought not to be segregated from that society but integrated into it and integrated also into its representation on television.

It is an argument which was succinctly put by Ruth Caleb, BBC drama producer. She chose the *Raspberry Ripple* script because 'it is not a play about being disabled but a play about somebody who wants to be regarded as a person within their own terms'. She continued:

> I don't know. I suspect that the disabled don't want to be treated as a cause ... I think they just want to work and not be discriminated against because they are not able-bodied ... I am not sure that more of the *Does He Take Sugar?* type of programme on the screen is actually going to be helpful.... What we want to give the audience is good viewing. If they go away asking a few questions about disability – good – but we don't want them to be thinking 'Oh God! I didn't realise how bad things are for the disabled!'
>
> (O'Neill, 1988, pp. 8–9)

The objection to television 'ghettos' for people with disabilities is well put, but it is important to note that such programmes may be valuable, especially to people with disabilities. Many of the people with disabilities interviewed for this project as well as those who had contact with people with disabilities did watch such programmes and found them of great value. Past research by the BBC confirms this view and also that such programmes are 'more likely' to be viewed by people with disabilities and carers than by the general population as a whole (BBC, 1986, p. 10). But people with disabilities also watch a considerable amount of other television and it is the general absence of 'adequate' and 'positive' portrayals across the range of programming which is at issue.

MORE OR BETTER REPRESENTATIONS

It may be useful here, as in Part I, to separate two arguments which run through the above discussion. The first deals with the 'statistical' representation of people with disabilities on television, and the second with the quality of the representations.

The statistical argument

There are two strands to this argument. First, there is the view that television should give a statistical representation of society. This has been fully discussed in Part I and needs no further examination here. The second strand also has already been identified and it reflects respondents' comments to the effect that people with disabilities are usually represented in certain ways (as cases for charity, pitiful, etc.) and usually appear in certain types of programmes (documentaries) but not others (for example, soaps). Members of the public, according to our survey of the audience, appeared equally aware of television's rather restricted register of disabled characters. The fact that television does not provide a representative picture of society was fully recognised by the public as a whole. Our survey, based on interviews with 1,016 respondents, showed that the public perceives that people with disabilities usually appear only in certain types of programmes. See Tables 7.1 to 7.3.

Any proper representation of society on television ought, the argument would run, to allow for similar proportions across the full range of television output.

Linked to this argument is a point which often came up in the discussions, namely, television's public service role as a social educator. To many, television was not a throw-away medium. It had to deal with these issues because they were important but also because it had a public service role to inform and educate. This is a conception of the role of television which may be eroded in the age of the new media.

The drawback to the statistical/reality argument is that it

Table 7.1 How often do people with disabilities appear in soap operas (percentages)?

	Often	Occasionally	Hardly ever	Never	No answer	Number
Total sample	3	21	38	27	2	1003
Respondent disabled	3	15	39	32	11	66
Respondent has disabled relative/friend	3	22	38	26	11	425
Respondent has no disabled relative/friend	3	20	38	28	11	576
Respondent works with disabled people	2	28	35	21	14	134
Respondent does not work with disabled people	3	19	39	28	11	867
Weight of viewing						
– Light	3	19	40	18	20	230
– Medium	2	23	36	27	12	381
– Heavy	4	19	39	32	5	392

Table 7.2 How often do people with disabilities appear in documentaries (percentages)?

	Often	Occasionally	Hardly ever	Never	No answer	Number
Total sample	34	51	9	3	3	1003
Respondent disabled	30	50	11	3	6	66
Respondent has disabled relative/friend	41	46	8	3	2	425
Respondent has no disabled relative/friend	29	54	9	4	4	576
Respondent works with disabled people	38	49	10	1	2	134
Respondent does not work with disabled people	34	51	8	3	4	867
Weight of viewing						
– Light	33	50	9	3	6	230
– Medium	38	51	6	2	2	381
– Heavy	32	50	10	4	3	392

Table 7.3 How often do people with disabilities appear in sitcoms (percentages)?

	Often	Occasionally	Hardly ever	Never	No answer	Number
Total sample	2	18	39	33	8	1003
Respondent disabled	2	24	26	41	8	66
Respondent has disabled relative/friend	2	19	41	31	7	425
Respondent has no disabled relative/friend	3	17	37	35	8	576
Respondent works with disabled people	2	19	39	26	13	134
Respondent does not work with disabled people	3	18	39	34	7	867
Weight of viewing						
– Light	3	17	37	28	14	230
– Medium	2	19	43	30	7	381
– Heavy	3	17	36	39	5	392

overlooks the simple point (illustrated in Chapter 2 above) that television does not mirror reality; it selects from the available material to suit its own requirements. This is not to condone the actions of television controllers but it is a reminder that television is first and foremost a medium of entertainment rather than a medium of 'social engineering'. To ask television to portray and employ more people with disabilities may be judicious and timely but it may not be easily reconciled with other demands made upon it.

The demand for 'positive' imagery

The demand for more 'positive' images is one that touches upon the quality of the representations rather than their quantity and frequency. This demand has clear parallels with the demands of other groups which feel themselves to be discriminated against or oppressed in relation to television, both in terms of employment opportunities and also in terms of representation. It is thus not surprising that references were often made to the position of blacks and women as well as gay people.

But what is a 'positive' image? Is it an image of a black person or a person with a disability which treats him/her as a person who is black/disabled almost without reference to his/her blackness/ disability, or is it a representation which takes up the issue of blackness/disability, calling attention to it and drawing strength from it? Simply put, do you draw attention to the disability or do you ignore it? It is that sort of problem that lies at the heart of Ruth Caleb's statement (see p. 97) and which affects producers' and public attitudes as well. And it is familiar to all who have followed a similar argument in relation to the treatment of black people in the mass media. For this reason, it is worth quoting at some length from a study of ethnic minorities and the media which highlights the same fundamental issue.

Hartmann and Husband, in their 1972 study of the frequency of appearances of blacks on television, concluded that

> the greater number of black faces on the [American television] screen did not therefore carry with it an increased exposure of black American culture. It would seem that blacks in American television drama are not functioning as representatives of any distinctive black culture; rather they are merely black skins in white roles. Their presence does not add materially to the nature

of the values which are displayed; they could in all honesty be replaced by white men.

Even when deliberate efforts are made to improve the presentation of black people on television, an inadequate analysis of the problem yields an inadequate solution. It is not a matter of greater frequency of presentation but a need for greater expression of black values and culture through television.

(p. 199)

The difficulty with simply increasing the quantity of appearances lay in the relationship between appearances and 'reality':

The close link between fact (blacks' low occupational status) and stereotype also imposes a limit on the extent to which a 'liberalisation' of media drama could upgrade the roles allocated to blacks. Any consistent upgrading would strain dramatic credibility because it presented a fake image of reality. Again it is apparent that real changes in the media presentation of blacks must be accompanied by a radical change in their position within the society itself.

(p. 203)

It is easy to see the nature of the difficulties which lie ahead. For Hartmann and Husband, the issue was not simply one of 'frequency' but one of 'quality', and that 'quality' had to allow for the expression of 'black values and culture' through television. It is worth pondering whether the same or similar demands are likely to be made by people with disabilities. The evidence to hand does suggest that the demand for greater frequency of appearances is certainly there, as is the demand for a more positive image. The demand for the representation of a disability culture can also be found in the literature, though it is not a demand that was made in any of the discussion groups. If anything, the major demands focused on the need for (greater) accessibility to all walks of life and for media representations which did not categorise and demean people with disabilities but which showed them as individuals (and groups) playing their part in society. As respondents put it:

We are very much like people who are retired early. They feel they are thrown on the scrap heap. We are virtually the same, only we have been retired through disability.

We must prove ourselves not only to ourselves but also to

others, but when you have a mass of people rushing at you to aid you, it rather negates your own determination and it enhances their preconceived ideas that we are helpless.

But we don't want to be helpless. We want to be useful.

Chapter 8

Public attitudes towards the portrayal of disability on television

This chapter will attempt to explore some of the issues outlined above in the context of a survey of the public conducted by the BBC on behalf of the Broadcasting Research Unit. Some of the data are referred to elsewhere, for example in Tables 7.1 to 7.3; here the remaining data are examined.

The questions posed in the questionnaire dealt with two broad areas: attitudes concerning the meaning of disability and attitudes to the portrayal of disability on television. The restricted space available in the survey questionnaire prevented us from dealing with either of these issues in depth; nevertheless there are sufficient data to indicate general patterns of thinking.

WHAT IS DISABILITY?

The first question asked of the 1,016 respondents was: 'When I say the word 'disabled', what do you think of?' This question was intended to elicit unprompted replies about 'disability'. It was left to the respondent to say what he/she thought. As expected, the responses were varied. They included the following:

A person who has lost the ability to use a limb or faculty.
People in wheelchairs and the mentally disabled.
Someone in a wheelchair.
People not with full functions, from somebody being slightly handicapped to paraplegic.
A person with physical or mental handicaps.

Most of the responses focused on the medical aspects of disability and disability as a condition due to a disabling characteristic.
Although there were minor variations between different groups,

these did not substantially alter the general pattern of response. For instance, while mobility concerned 28 per cent of the 55 + -year-olds, it was mentioned by only 16 per cent of the 16–24-year-olds. Mobility was more often mentioned by DEs[1] (29 per cent) than by ABs (19 per cent); the opposite was the case for blindness (36 per cent of AB responses, 20 per cent DE) and deafness (28 per cent AB, 13 per cent DE). There were no large differences between men and women.

We also looked for differences between respondents with disabilities, the 'able-bodied', and professional or voluntary carers for those with disabilities.

Of the 1,016 respondents, 39 said that they were registered disabled, blind or deaf and 45 said that they had some permanent disability. Given that these answers overlapped, the survey actually identified 67 respondents (or 7 per cent of the total sample) who can be considered to be disabled in some way, a number which allows only for some general comparisons between different groups.

The survey also sought to find out how many respondents had a close relative or friend with a disability, or worked with people with disabilities. Of the total sample of 1,016, 430 (or 42 per cent) answered that they had a close relative or friend who had a disability, and 134 (or 13 per cent) said that they worked with disabled people.

The point at issue was whether these different groups would respond differently to the questions posed. As regards the general question regarding the meaning of disability, the responses were not significantly different (see Table 8.1).

What is most evident from the responses is that the 'social model' is not so much in the minds of members of the public as to be articulated readily when a question is asked about the meaning of 'disability'. Members of the public evidently see 'the disabled' as individuals who need help because of a medical condition.

The survey attempted to explore this issue further by asking respondents to distinguish between those medical conditions which they thought were, or were not, disabilities.

The question had two main objectives. First, it attempted to identify the problem of 'inclusion and exclusion': who defines the meaning of disability and who is disabled, and whose definitions do we accept? The second objective was to assess whether the public held the view that every condition named (medical or otherwise) was 'disabling'. It will be recalled that these positions were outlined by many in the discussion groups which were made up of people with disabilities or carers. Table 8.2 sets out the responses, broken down

Table 8.1 When I say the word 'disabled', what do you think of
(percentages)?

	Sample	Disabled	Knew someone disabled
	N = 1016	67	430
Wheelchair	34	29	35
Mobility or movement difficulties	22	27	20
Limbs malformed, missing, deficient	14	14	13
Blind	27	17	31
Deaf	20	8	23
Physical handicap	17	5	18
Mental handicap	17	9	20
Handicapped/can't do something	24	18	25
People who need help	5	5	4
Cerebral palsy	2	2	3
Down's Syndrome	*	0	1
MS	1	0	2
Epilepsy	*	0	*
Diabetes	*	0	*
Spina Bifida	*	2	*
Arthritis	1	2	1
Asthma	*	3	*
Parkinson's Disease	0	0	0
Autism	*	*	*
Leukaemia	0	0	0
Speech impairment	2	0	2
Others/Don't know/ No answer	15	32	15

* indicates less than 1%
Note: As this was an open-ended question, more than one response was coded

by groups: those who were disabled, those who have a close relative
or friend who is disabled and those who work with disabled people.

Briefly, between 80 per cent and 90 per cent of every category
answered that the following were disabilities: missing or malformed
limbs, total deafness (partial deafness was considered a disability by
about 50 per cent of each group), blindness (partial blindness was
considered a disability by over 60 per cent of each group), mental
handicaps, mobility problems. There are no significant differences
according to age, sex or class in these responses.

About half of the sample acknowledged that 'restricted growth' is

Table 8.2 Is it a disability (percentages)?

	Disability	Not a disability	Don't know/ it varies	N
(a) Being in a wheelchair				
Total sample	92	6	2	1016
Respondent disabled	94	4	2	67
Respondent has disabled relative/ friend	92	6	3	430
Respondent works with disabled people	93	6	2	134
(b) Epilepsy				
Total sample	56	38	7	1016
Respondent disabled	58	37	4	67
Respondent has disabled relative/ friend	53	38	9	430
Respondent works with disabled people	60	34	6	134
(c) Severe short sight				
Total sample	50	45	5	1016
Respondent disabled	55	39	6	67
Respondent has disabled relative/ friend	52	43	4	430
Respondent works with disabled people	64	32	2	134
(d) Cerebral Palsy				
Total sample	93	5	2	1016
Respondent disabled	97	1	1	67
Respondent has disabled relative/ friend	93	4	3	430
Respondent works with disabled people	94	4	2	134
(e) Diabetes				
Total sample	24	71	5	1016
Respondent disabled	34	57	9	67
Respondent has disabled relative/ friend	24	72	4	430
Respondent works with disabled people	29	66	4	134

a disability, and half did not. Migraine, diabetes and depression were considered disabilities by some 30 per cent of each group. Scars were more problematic, since about 70 per cent of the population consider this not to be a disability while only 55 per cent of those who are disabled see it that way.

As with many of the responses, it is difficult to speculate on the differences between those who are disabled and the sample as a whole. It could be that people with disabilities are more aware and more sympathetic to those whose life is inconvenienced by a physical condition whose consequences are dramatic.

The responses highlight the physical/medical definition of disability and, equally important, the uncertainty expressed over some 'disabilities', such as epilepsy and diabetes, which are usually included under the general umbrella term. Is this because there is a common view that if the condition can be controlled medically or is usually invisible, it should not be classed alongside the more commonly accepted disabilities?

The data are inconclusive but there are other data that lend support to the perception of the disabled as a group that is partially dependent rather than independent and that needs care rather than being able to fend for itself. Again, this is certainly related to how one conceives of disability. If one conceives of disability as a dis-abling condition – as with the severely mentally handicapped – then it is difficult to argue that they can lead independent lives. The same would be true of those suffering from severe multiple sclerosis (MS) or paraplegia. Conversely, if the notion of disability brings to mind people suffering from epilepsy or diabetes, then one's response will take a different form.

The data at hand are limited, but they do, nevertheless, provide no evidence for any public inclination toward the 'social model' and its central tenet that it is 'society which disables'. The greater proportion of the public – and not only the 'able-bodied' public – appears to take the view that it is medical conditions that 'disable' (whether or not 'society' disables further).

As Table 8.3 shows, about 60 per cent of each category agrees either a lot or a little with the statement 'most disabled people can live normal lives', and 26 per cent disagree, either a little or a lot.

When the sense of the statement was reversed into 'most disabled people need a great deal of help in order to live normal lives', 63 per cent of respondents in all categories agreed that they did need help, while only 24 per cent disagreed. The full figures are given in the table.

Table 8.3 What kind of life (percentages)?

	Agree a lot	Agree a little	Neither	Disagree a little	Disagree a lot	No answer	N
(a) 'Most disabled people can live normal lives.'							
Total sample	26	35	11	17	9	2	1003
Respondent disabled	29	33	12	14	11	2	66
Respondent has disabled relative/friend	30	35	8	17	9	0	425
Respondent has no disabled relative/friend	23	35	13	17	8	3	576
Respondent works with disabled people	23	36	11	18	12	0	134
Respondent does not work with disabled people	27	35	11	17	8	2	867
(b) 'Most disabled people need a great deal of help in order to live normal lives.'							
Total sample	30	33	11	19	5	2	1003
Respondent disabled	29	35	11	20	3	3	66
Respondent has disabled relative/friend	33	31	10	19	6	1	425
Respondent has no disabled relative/friend	28	35	12	18	4	3	576
Respondent works with disabled people	29	28	10	22	8	2	134
Respondent does not work with disabled people	30	34	12	18	4	2	867

Table 8.4 Too much or too little portrayal of disability (percentages)?

	Agree a lot	Agree a little	Neither	Disagree a little	Disagree a lot	No answer	N
(a) 'There are too many dramas and soap operas which feature people with disabilities.'							
Total sample	1	3	6	23	59	8	1003
Respondent disabled	3	3	6	14	62	12	66
Respondent has disabled relative/friend	0	2	7	20	64	8	425
Respondent has no disabled relative/friend	2	3	6	25	56	9	576
Respondent works with disabled people	0	4	6	20	60	10	134
Respondent does not work with disabled people	1	3	6	23	59	8	867
(b) 'There are too few dramas and soap operas on television which feature people with disabilities.'							
Total sample	33	27	15	10	7	9	1003
Respondent disabled	32	23	11	8	15	13	66
Respondent has disabled relative/friend	37	25	15	8	6	9	425
Respondent has no disabled relative/friend	30	28	15	10	7	10	576
Respondent works with disabled people	34	29	11	7	6	12	134
Respondent does not work with disabled people	33	26	15	10	7	8	867

The responses suggest that the public view people with disabilities as being to some extent dependent on the services of others. The physical conditions impose their own requirements. Thus, while opponents of racism and sexism can point to the absence of real substantive differences between people, critics of 'handicappism' appear to ignore or underplay those differences which are both real and have real consequences.

These points are pertinent to the discussion of the OPCS report (above, pp. 92–3). To criticise it for adopting the medical model of disability is valid only if the medical model has no application to people with disabilities. That it can be applied, and that public responses reflect this, limits the scope of the criticisms. However, there may be something deeper lying behind these responses and the responses of many of the disabled discussants to the effect that they want independence to run their own lives. It could be that the general public does not understand well the true meaning of disability; that it still only sees the disability rather than the person. Nevertheless, that even carers do not diverge from the general direction of the responses in Table 8.3 suggests that the critics have a long way to go to develop public understanding. But it remains valid to claim that the 'social model' can deepen understanding of the condition of people with disabilities, even if it cannot, as often suggested, fully explain it.

What is the public response to other issues concerning 'television and disablement'?

In Chapter 7 we pointed out that the public was well aware of the paucity of appearances by people with disabilities in different types of television genres. The survey contained two statements which allow us to check the public's consistency in their responses. Thus, 82 per cent of most of the groups disagreed either a lot or a little with the statement 'there are too many drama and soap programmes which feature people with disabilities'. The one exception was the group of disabled respondents in which a lower proportion (76 per cent) disagreed either a lot or a little with the statement.

When the statement was reversed into 'there are too few drama programmes on television which feature people with disabilities', so too were the answers. Sixty per cent agreed either a little or a lot with the statement that there were too few programmes featuring disabled people; 55 per cent of disabled respondents also agreed with the statement. Some 15 per cent of the total sample neither agreed nor disagreed. So, while most disagreed with the view that there were too many programmes featuring people with disabilities, most agreed that there were too few and a large number gave neither a positive nor a negative response.

Should people with disabilities appear in a range of programmes or should they be restricted to certain categories of programmes? Table 8.5 explores this question.

Seventy-one per cent or more of the respondents felt that people with disabilities should appear in all types of programmes. Fewer disabled respondents were so definite; 68 per cent agreed a little or a lot with that statement. It is also worth noting that 17 per cent of respondents in most categories (except those who work with the disabled) disagreed a little or a lot with the statement and that 11 per cent of respondents were neutral, neither agreeing nor disagreeing. One may conclude then that a majority of the public does believe that people with disabilities should appear across all genres. Again, when the statement is in part reversed, so are the responses, but this time they are somewhat more positive. Over 80 per cent of respondents (79 per cent in the case of the disabled respondents) felt that people with disabilities should not be restricted to their own programmes.

Finally, an attempt was made to assess the view expressed by television producers and controllers in interview that the viewing public would find people with disabilities on television embarrassing, disturbing and/or distressing.

A small minority agreed either a little or a lot with the statement: 'I sometimes get embarrassed seeing severely disabled people on television.' Interestingly, 23 per cent of disabled respondents agreed a little or a lot with the statement, as opposed to under 20 per cent of other groups of respondents; only 15 per cent of those who worked with people with disabilities agreed (a little or a lot) with the statement. Conversely, whilst 74 per cent disagreed a little or a lot with the statement, only 66 per cent of the disabled did so. It may be said, as many group discussants did, that it is the respondent's problem if he/she feels embarrassed, but there appears to be a sizeable body of opinion here to be taken into account.

A similar set of responses were given to a statement which sought to find out if the public felt that some disabilities were 'too disturbing and should not be shown on television'. Here again, disabled respondents were out of step with the majority (see Table 8.6). While 37 per cent of the total sample agreed a lot or a little with that statement, 46 per cent of the disabled respondents did so. Conversely, while 56 per cent disagreed a little or a lot with the statement, only 37 per cent of disabled respondents did so. Admittedly, 15 per cent of disabled respondents neither agreed nor disagreed but the general pattern suggests that people with disabilities are slightly more likely than others to feel embarrassed or disturbed by appearances of people with disabilities.

Table 8.5 People with disabilities should appear in all types of programmes (percentages)

	Agree a lot	Agree a little	Neither	Disagree a little	Disagree a lot	No answer	N
Total sample	43	28	11	13	4	2	1003
Respondent disabled	48	20	12	14	2	3	66
Respondent has disabled relative/friend	49	24	11	11	3	0	425
Respondent has no disabled relative/friend	39	30	10	14	5	3	576
Respondent works with disabled people	53	25	10	8	3	1	134
Respondent does not work with disabled people	42	28	11	14	4	2	867

Table 8.6 Some disabilities are too disturbing and should not be shown on television

	Agree a lot	Agree a little	Neither	Disagree a little	Disagree a lot	No answer	N
Total sample	13	24	7	17	36	2	1003
Respondent disabled	16	30	15	11	26	3	66
Respondent has disabled relative/friend	12	21	6	18	41	1	425
Respondent has no disabled relative/friend	14	26	7	16	33	3	576
Respondent works with disabled people	12	23	7	10	46	1	134
Respondent does not work with disabled people	14	24	7	18	35	3	867

Chapter 9

The employment of disabled actors

Should disabled characters be played by actors with disabilities? The simplicity of this question belies the complex issues which it raises, for it is not just a matter of actors taking specific roles; it also involves the matter of positive discrimination, the availability and suitability of actors with disabilities, the opportunities for these actors to obtain training and experience and, lastly, the availability of roles for actors with disabilities.

There is not much doubt that most television producers and writers would answer the question in the affirmative. Yet most also point out the difficulties which they encounter in attempting to fulfil this objective. Access to studios, costs and the availability of suitable actors to play the parts are only some of the obstacles mentioned. There appears to be no lack of sympathy but a feeling, or realisation, that the odds are stacked against them if they attempt to achieve their goal. One producer remarked that for many producers, the 'first reaction would be to get an actor to sit in a wheelchair, though I would personally think of getting someone in a wheelchair'.

For some, this issue is not particularly important but for many others it goes to the heart of the matter. The latter would argue forcefully that it does matter whether or not a character with a disability is played by an actor who is disabled. Clearly, there are instances when this would not be possible but, by and large, actors with disabilities should be allowed to play the appropriate parts; in the words of one interviewee, 'they would bring their own personal experiences to the part'.

Such a position is often given support by drawing parallels with the plight of black actors. Nowadays, few would even think of casting a white actor to play a black part and, by extension, one might suppose that able-bodied actors would rarely be cast to play disabled characters. This sort of argument is used to counter those who put forward the view that since acting is all about pretence, extending the pretence in such instances is quite logical. Although there is a rationale for this view, it fails to take into account the fact that the reverse is not true, namely, that actors with disabilities (or black actors) are rarely if ever given the opportunity to play roles usually taken by able-bodied (or white) actors.

In other words, this debate needs to be seen in the broader context of the opportunities which are or are not available to actors with disabilities. To this one clearly needs to add the question of acting ability, but this is something that makes sense only within the broader context; for, unless actors with disabilities obtain sufficient experience to master their profession, it will always be possible for producers to claim that there was no suitable candidate.

At the present time, it seems to be true that the majority of characters with a disability portrayed on television are played by able-bodied actors. Programmes where characters with disabilities have appeared recently – *The Return of Shelley*, *Rockliffe's Babies*, *Call Me Mister*, *Taggart* – confirm this generalisation, though only a more exhaustive analysis would settle the question finally.

So why do producers and directors cast able-bodied actors as disabled characters? The question of 'suitability' certainly comes into it. One producer remarked that he had tried enormously hard to find an actor with a disability to play a particular role but that in the end he had to cast an able-bodied person in the part as others were not quite right. 'Suitability' may mean that the actor is considered unable to cope with the full range of situations required of him/her. Some of these limitations can be attributable to a disability per se or they may be the result of inexperience. Sometimes it may not be appropriate to cast a disabled actor to play a severely disabled character. The examples quoted during the research included a character with advanced MS and a character who was mentally handicapped. In both cases it might not have been possible to get the performances required, assuming that actors with these disabilities were available.

Such difficulties should not be underestimated and they do create problems for all those involved, problems which have to be resolved if the production is to be completed. In the case of Nina in *Crossroads*, for instance, they had to write the plot with some variations in case Nina did not act as required; they had, in other words, to anticipate impromptu changes to scenes. It could be that reasons such as these may only disguise an unwillingness to take on 'unknown factors', but they do none the less suggest that some unease about the suitability and the capabilities of actors with disabilities is real.

Another reason for casting an able-bodied actor could be that he/she may be an asset to the production and its sales potential whereas an actor with a disability might be an unknown and thus a less attractive proposition. There are two other considerations which are often conflated with this reason and both raise problems for actors with disabilities. The first relates to the opportunities for actors with disabilities to train in their art. If they are excluded from television, how can they show their skills and how will they then be noticed? The second reason is closely allied to this. Where are the opportunities for training actors with disabilities in mainstream theatre and television? Unless such actors are granted access to the 'windows of opportunity', they will not be able to break into the wider media world. The circle is both vicious and closed.

It should also be borne in mind that unless actors with disabilities are given the opportunity to play any roles which do not specifically require a disabled actor, they are in danger of being restricted to a very small register of parts. The parallels with black actors are again pertinent. One should not cast a black actor simply because he/she is black and the part requires it; rather, if the part does not require any special traits, all should have the opportunity to play it.

As BBC producer Ruth Caleb commented:

> One often casts able-bodied people in disabled parts. Why can't we cast disabled people in able-bodied parts. There is no reason why a barman can't be a disabled barman or a vicar can't be a disabled vicar.... I am not sure I could ever argue for positive discrimination because I do not think that to argue for positive discrimination is ever really a valid argument. I think it has to be left to individual producers and directors and making them aware of what the problem is, and then I think that if there are good actors, they will be used.
>
> (O'Neill, 1988, p. 18)

Caleb touches on one theme which cannot be ignored, that of positive discrimination. Although most discussants felt that disabled actors ought to be employed wherever possible, there were reservations about making this compulsory. The belief that actors should be chosen on merit rather than because they are disabled is a difficult one to abandon, and it was often reflected in people's comments. 'Yes, it is important that actors with disabilities be chosen but it is crucial that they also merit the part' paraphrases many of the comments made in the discussion groups. That this position creates obstacles for actors with disabilities is not ignored, but it needs to be seen alongside the desire to be treated just like everyone else and not as individuals who merit special favours.

Another possible reason for not using actors with disabilities could be that there are insufficient actors to take on these roles. Equity's register of disabled actors is not a large one. It currently comprises about one hundred names, though some actors with disabilities are cited in its main register. This may make it difficult to cast actors with disabilities since the likelihood of exactly the right sort of actor being available may be small.

The fact that some actors with disabilities refuse to be included in Equity's register narrows down the list of names one can immediately turn to. However, existing theatre companies which are made up of actors with disabilities, such as Graeae, do provide training for such actors and, perhaps more importantly, a ready source of names for producers. Informal networks of this kind are undoubtedly important but they cannot overcome the lack of opportunity and training facilities for actors with disabilities.

If these difficulties were not enough, there are some other ready-made answers to the initial question. These point to the economic dimension of television: put at its simplest, with a tight schedule, a limited budget and inaccessible rehearsal facilities it may not be feasible to take on a disabled actor. Facilities without access for, say, wheelchairs rule out chairbound actors; actors who are hard of hearing may need someone to sign for them; actors who are blind may be difficult to direct and so on. It is television's version of 'fire regulations' – why take on these extra problems?

As one producer explained:

Had the setting been different it would have been easier to rehearse but the rehearsal rooms had inadequate facilities and it was not clear whether I would get clearance to use a disabled actor, to provide extra transport and so on....

If it was essential that I use a disabled actor because it had been written there, I would do it but again I have the time factor to take into account. [With such a tight schedule of rehearsals and filming]

I couldn't take on an unknown factor. I could take on any disabled actor if they could act the part within the confines I have with regard to recording, other actors' commitments, sets, and so on.

If I had the luxury of, say, x weeks per programme then 'yes'... but the networks demand that you get things ready as quickly as possible.

These points were not universally accepted. One producer said bluntly:

Absolute balls ... just bullshit. We rehearse where we want to and all the studios have double doors for moving sets. We have no problems at all. No problems with acting as such and I have no problems getting actors.

Admittedly, this producer was primarily concerned with children's drama but his statement was applied to the range of television output. Moreover, it was a view which found a measure of support from Ruth Caleb:

The disabled artists we used [in *Raspberry Ripple*] were very keen to point out that they wanted no concessions for their disability and so they would be prepared to work a 13-hour day, often in difficult conditions. They were at pains to point out that just because they were disabled, it does not mean we have to give them the kid-glove treatment. The only thing they had to watch out for were steps – their accessibility to locations and to loos.

A final reason why actors with disabilities might not be used takes us back to the example of Nina in *Crossroads* and the sorts of difficulties encountered by Nabil Shaban over *Microman*: are actors with disabilities too 'distressing' for the ordinary viewer to watch? Would they upset the sensibilities of the viewing audience? In the case of *Microman*, Shaban explained that although no reasons were given for aborting the project,

I had my suspicions. I already knew that a certain head of drama at Granada had stated in an interview that he did not envisage a disabled actor playing the role in a TV programme. When asked to consider the possibility of a disabled performer in the cast of *Coronation Street* Granada had said a definite 'No'.

Knowing of these two outright prejudices, I 'phoned the producer [of *Microman*]. He immediately admitted that the Granada executive producers were worried that many children would find me frightening, ie that they would be frightened when seeing someone as disabled as me in a wheelchair in such a dominant role.

He continued:

> Thus Granada did not want to take the risk. If it was a one-off they might have done, but a seven-parter? No way!
>
> (O'Neill, 1988, pp. 36–7)

As noted, there was a belief that Shaban would have had a negative reaction from the audience. Whether this would be justified either because of his physical appearance or because one just does not cast an actor with a disability in a leading role is not particularly important when producers believe that it would somehow not be the appropriate thing to do.

Certainly, the experience of Nina in *Crossroads* does suggest that the public is not as open-minded as one might like to assume. While she was on the soap, there were many letters in the press and to the producer and the writer critical of the episodes in question. Many of these letters objected to her appearance on such a programme and at such a time (early evening), and many objected to the sight of the disability itself, claiming that they did not particularly wish to view such a disability on their favourite programmes. In the cuttings files, one can also find reference to ratings declining (though this has yet to be substantiated).

According to someone who was very closely involved in these programmes, there was certainly a feeling that there would be immense difficulties if the person chosen to play the part of Nina was not 'the acceptable face of handicap'. As he pointed out:

> it had to be the acceptable face of handicap because it went out at tea-time. You could not have a person who slobbers, which is also the reality of mental handicap. Whilst we felt that we were educating the public about mental handicap, there was a danger that we were not educating them as fully as we ought to do.
>
> We tried to counteract that a little and we felt that we had a job to get the reality over to the viewers because there was a danger that viewers would believe that it was all very easy and no problem (as it might have appeared on television).

It could be that one disability is more 'visually acceptable' than another; it could also be that the audience felt that it was being preached to; it could be that the 'reality' of the Down's Syndrome child somehow destroyed the fictional reality of the soap. After all, one could not turn to one's child and claim that it was 'someone dressed up'. It required an explanation of fact and a comprehension of disability; it was, in this sense, a confrontation with the uncomfortable.

Although one producer objected to the view that the audience should be insulated from the range of 'unattractive' disabilities, he did go on to say that even he and his team spent three weeks debating whether a certain person with a severe disability should be shown on screen. In the end they did show that particular boy, but the producer was unhappy that there was no backup or support to explain matters to those who needed explanations to further their understanding. One could easily confront the audience, but if one wanted to help the audience to understand the disability better – to help the parent explain to the child, say – one needed something more. And that something was not available through television.

Chapter 10

A closer look at responses to the portrayal of disability on television

Whether one adopts a medical or a social model of disability, one thing emerged very clearly during this research. Members of the public (including members of the discussion groups) were able to identify a wide range of disabilities and most of these were readily placed under the general heading of 'disability'. One consequence of this is that when discussants were asked, 'when did you last see a person with a disability on television?', the answers were plentiful and covered an enormous range of conditions: cerebral palsy, amputation, disfigurement, dyslexia, Down's Syndrome, being wheelchair-bound and so on. Admittedly, such a range of examples emerged gradually. The first answer would prompt another example, then another and so on. In one instance, for example, one discussant mentioned the case of Nina in *Crossroads* and this was followed within several minutes by contributions from others: an Asian comedian with cerebral palsy; an epileptic boy; a boy with dyslexia; a Down's Syndrome child on an Australian soap; a mentally handicapped man; and an autistic man.

Such a response from one discussion group – and others gave a similarly broad range – would appear at first sight contrary to the general unease expressed about television's limited portrayal of people with disability. As Part I has shown, people with disabilities are not, in fact, absent from the screen; yet public perception is quite different. Generally speaking, all the interviewees emphasised the low number of appearances and not their frequency.

There are two possible reasons for this anomaly. One is that we are not *consciously* aware of the appearance of characters with disabilities; we could be watching a drama or a comedy programme when someone who is disabled appears ... but we somehow 'screen' them out or do not take them in, and cannot readily recall them. This is a point made by Longmore (1987) and it does appear plausible. We are not always conscious of all the characters in programmes. There may be a parallel here with studies of audience recall of news programmes, which suggest that actual recall of news items is rather low unless viewers are particularly interested in specific items and/or are prompted to recall items (see Robinson and Levy, 1986).

A related reason is that we may not directly connect these instances with disability and related issues. Such a reaction probably applied to viewing programmes such as *Ironside* where the more acute experiences of disability are absent. We are merely viewing a television programme and the fact of the disability is not a significant feature.

Perhaps more important than the ability to recall instances when people with disabilities have appeared on the screen was the varied reaction to programmes or television items which featured people with disabilities. Some people – particularly if they had no direct contact with people with disabilities – felt no compulsion or interest to watch such programmes. After watching a clip of Nina in *Crossroads* one young man said,

> That would be turned off. It's not my type of programme. It makes me feel sick to watch other people when you can do things and they can't.

Another said:

> We're all under 20, we don't want to sit down and watch these people. But [watching these people] you are also bored or sorry.

Yet these very same people admitted to watching (and enjoying) both *The Boy David* and *The Terry Fox Show*. It could be that they related to two young men who were in their age cohort; it could be that the storyline – overcoming adversity – was preferable to the *Crossroads* storyline and, for them, more immediate and identifiable. The reactions from the young people's group varied to such an extent that no generalisations are possible.

Interestingly enough, those members of group discussions who had some contact with people with disabilities reacted very differently to the very same scenes from *Crossroads*. On the whole, they found the scenes sensitively executed, 'realistic' and touching; these scenes, many felt, accurately portrayed the 'problems' of having a Down's Syndrome child. One obvious explanation of the different reactions is that the young people's group had had no contact with people with disabilities while the other groups had. Differences in age may also be important; the young able-bodied may be very different on this account from the carers and the parents of children with disabilities.

Two final points need to be made about Nina in *Crossroads* and both are critical. The first is a general one. One person who had been heavily involved in the making of the programmes with Nina felt that although the programmes were important and the character well created, using Nina in the programme was portraying 'the attractive side of disability'. She was 'a sweet-looking girl' who would be seen sympathetically; yet, conversely, she might also detract from the range of the real and the 'unattractive' disabilities portrayed. This criticism highlights the difficulty the media have in representing any and every facet of life. They necessarily choose to focus on topics and characters, and choices mean that certain things are included and others excluded ... choosing Nina meant not choosing someone else. Moreover, choosing Nina also meant choosing someone who was attractive and not someone else who was less attractive.

The other criticism is more specific and relates to one of the scenes shown to the discussion groups. It was a scene which caused some anxiety. It took place in a schoolroom. The children, all Down's Syndrome children, were singing along with their teacher. While they are singing and tapping their feet, the camera sweeps across the room and catches a young girl sitting on a potty. She is also taking part in the singing and foot stomping.

To some of the viewers this scene was touching and 'realistic'; in no way could it have been set up, since the whole scene was evidently being shot in the 'fly on the wall' tradition. But to many others, particularly to some of those with disabilities and some of their carers, it denied that young girl her privacy and was therefore unacceptable. As it would not be done to 'normal' children, it should not have been done to a child with Down's Syndrome. The issue of the media reflecting 'reality' also arises here, for some felt that if the scene had been recorded faithfully, that is, if she was sitting on the potty, then it should not have been edited out; that if things happen, they must not be denied.

The extent to which each and every representation can be questioned from different perspectives can also be seen in the next example. Again, it is worth relating in some detail because it touches on some of the main issues.

The programme in question was a recent edition of *Umbrella*, a programme which is built around the theme of religious education and the celebration of religious differences. In this programme the theme was perceptions and expectations, for example, that you may assume that blond people have blue eyes but this is not always so. The presenter then introduced a report with words to the effect of, 'if I mentioned an outward bound course you would think of the able-bodied ... but this one is different'.

There then followed a filmed report about an outward bound centre in the Lake District where children with disabilities are shown sailing, riding, abseiling and so on. There were two other elements in the film that are worth noting and both came in for criticism: the first was that the commentary consisted of the team leaders and organisers discussing and describing the centre and what it provides; the second was that the background music, a pop song, was called 'The Power of Love'. The connotations of the latter are abundantly clear – all this is possible because of, and with, love. But it is the former element which drew more attention. It was not so much that those concerned – people with disabilities or people who had contact with people with disabilities – did not enjoy watching children with disabilities doing things which are usually not available to them, but that the children on the film were never addressed and were never asked to say anything. It was yet another instance of the disabled being treated, intentionally or not, as if 'they were less than human'.

The ambivalence felt towards this item was clear. On the one hand it was good to see young children enjoying themselves but, on the other hand, it was reprehensible that they were not given the opportunity to describe their own feelings. Similarly, it was good to see young people given access to a wide range of facilities but it was rather sad that the facilities were segregated from others available to the wider community. After all, if the objective is for people with disabilities to be given full access to social processes or to be 'integrated' into society, images which emphasise segregation serve further to exclude people with disabilities.

Numerous discussants pointed out that there was little room within dramatic fiction for sensitive portrayals of almost anything. There is usually little room for emphasising the 'ordinary'. As one blind discussant admitted, 'there is nothing in our lives which would seem to interest television people'.

This view would seem unduly pessimistic. Fiction and its investigation of human conflict and interaction is surely not confined to able-bodied concerns. Furthermore, even if the focus were primarily on the able-bodied the likelihood is that at some point such characters would have some contact with disabled people.

Yet it is this exclusion from dramatic life that is most evident. And it is simply a degree of inclusion that people with disabilities demand; not necessarily as main characters, though that would not be unwelcome, but as individuals who have a part to play in the world of television fiction: as members of soaps, as participants in situation comedies, as office workers in police stations, as teachers, as parents, as commuters, as extras ... and so on.

The incorporation of the 'ordinary' into daily television practices has proved immensely difficult. What accounts for this absence? One answer touches on the nature of the television medium and its genres. Shorn of its trimmings, each genre tends to provide a basic formula to which writers and producers adhere. This could be regarded as a framework into which elements are added for the creation of different episodes of series or serials. Where this is the case writers seldom challenge contemporary assumptions and expectations. As John Ellis, an independent producer, writes:

> The series ... provides a stable situation in which various incidents take place week by week. The incidents usually form a complete group each week (except in the case of a soap opera).... A fundamental stability and return to zero at the end of each programme or programme section is implied by the series.
>
> The series is based upon the notion 'what will happen to them this week?'; known elements are repeated with no discernible development from one episode to the next.
>
> (Ellis, 1982, pp. 124–5)

A situation comedy, for example, does not leave much room for manoeuvre. The main characters have to remain constant in order to provide for the 'comforting continuity' which is a reason for its success.

Until television producers are ready to cast people with disabilities in leading roles, such characters will make only occasional appearances.

This does not mean that some portrayals, even if only as minor characters, cannot be sensitive and satisfactory. One series which was well received was *Taggart*, which features a wheelchair-bound woman as Taggart's wife. Although she was not the main character, she was close to him and, more importantly, she was portrayed as an independent person in her own right. She was a woman and a wife who had a disability rather than a disabled person. Such sensitive and commendable portrayals are probably rare and very much depend on the writers' abilities; more often than not, people with disabilities have 'one-off' appearances as minor characters.

In contrast to the restrictive environment provided by the series or serial, the one-off play or the dramatic feature provides ample room for writers and producers to break with convention, to develop characters, to play with difficult and complex ideas. As one writer put it: 'There is a world of difference between writing and filling in the words within a format.'

This freedom is even greater in the context of programmes which have an educational dimension. This partly – although only partly – explains why the portrayal of characters is so different across genres and across the flow of television programmes. The more room for manoeuvre, the more time for casting and rehearsals, the greater the depth and sensitivity of the end product. The other part of the explanation relates to the commitment and determination of the producers and writers to proceed with difficult ideas. This will be explored more fully below.

The inflexibility of the genre can be illustrated with reference to an episode in the series *The Return of Shelley*, an episode which was shown during the period of the content analysis and has already been discussed in Chapter 4. When shown to some of the discussion groups, it was, on the whole, well received: it was liked, people felt that it reflected their concerns well and that it portrayed the problems of being chair-bound accurately, using humour to drive the lessons home. Nevertheless, as an episode it touches on many issues discussed above: genre, choice of actors, the adequacy of the portrayal and so on.

Shelley is an unemployed graduate, a loner with a sharp tongue. In this particular episode it is his 42nd birthday. He is alone in his flat dictating his thoughts into a cassette recorder. A few minutes into the episode, his landlady and her boyfriend enter the scene and after a brief exchange invite him to their local wine bar.

Whilst drinking at the wine bar, a man in a wheelchair, Dave, enters and settles down at one of the many empty tables. The manager objects and there follows a conversation between the two to the effect that he, the manager, cannot have people in wheelchairs in the wine bar because of 'fire regulations'. Shelley intervenes, stressing the ludicrousness of the manager's reasoning, and, in solidarity with Dave, leaves the bar with him.

They adjourn to a local café where they are served alcoholic drinks in teapots.

The episode ends in Shelley's flat where he, Dave and several other individuals whom they have picked up along the way celebrate the last remaining hours of his birthday.

What is obvious from this episode is that the disabled character is a 'one off'. To paraphrase Ellis, he is part of what is going to happen to them this week.

The uniqueness of the appearance should not be taken as a criticism of the intentions of the writer or as evidence of the failure of the episode. As mentioned above, it was an episode which was well received and the lines delivered by the actor in the wheelchair appeared to connect with the personal experiences of those who were familiar with the problems of access for the disabled. However, the uniqueness of the appearance does reinforce the dominance of the able-bodied, a pattern that is disrupted only fleetingly by Dave, the man in the wheelchair. One could also argue that this character, along with the others picked up along the way, are all 'losers' or 'failures' in one way or another and that this only goes to confirm the supremacy of the able-bodied.

The one major criticism which was made of the programme again highlights the problems of dealing with a difficult area. Several discussants felt that the writer and producer took the easy way out by letting Shelley and Dave leave the wine bar. They in effect bowed to discrimination. These discussants felt that the issue should have been confronted directly and not swept away.

It is important to add that this view was not a universal one; indeed many felt that the use of humour allowed the iniquity of the situation to shine through without the viewer being preached at. In fact, 'preaching' might have been counterproductive because it would have alerted the viewer to a didactic use of television.

The more general point to make in the context of the present discussion is that to attempt to go beyond the occasional appearance of a disabled character it would be necessary to break with convention and write the main character as a character with a disability, as in *Ironside*. But this would have to be written in such a way that the character's disability is not primarily, or perhaps even only, a dramatic device. It would have to reflect the ordinariness of the situation as well as its capture of reality. In other words, it could not be made up of a preposterous plot or it would be 'unbelievable'. It is this sort of problem which Hartmann and Husband (1972) identified in relation to the portrayal of blacks.

Given the limitations of television genres, it is not surprising that most interviewees felt that the only way to overcome the rather negative portrayals of people with disabilities was to include such people in the soap opera format. The reasons for this are fairly straightforward. The soap allows characters to develop; it would thus allow long-term exposure to a character with a disability and give writers – and actors – the opportunity to touch on a number of issues that are at present neglected. Equally important is the fact that soaps are watched by many millions who might then become used to people with disabilities in an 'everyday' setting. As discussed above, attempts to introduce disabled characters into contemporary soaps have not been very successful. *Brookside* featured a young boy with dyslexia, as well as a young man, Owen, wheelchair-bound after a car accident (after our sample period), and *Eastenders* featured a character diagnosed as having MS, although he, as many discussants noted, has vanished from the series, as indeed has Owen from *Brookside*.

Attempts to break with the conventions of television are rarely encouraged. Those who have tried to do new things have often had their paths blocked. The example of the aborted programme *Microman* which was to have featured Nabil Shaban comes readily to mind, as does the case of a plan to produce a children's series based around characters in wheelchairs. Both series met with disfavour, although it is worth adding that the latter will now be produced, albeit not by the original commissioning company.

Many reasons have been put forward to explain these refusals. There was a general feeling among controllers of television that it was somehow not 'appropriate'. Thus,

> I wanted a feature part for someone with a disability but it met with a fairly lukewarm response.

or,

I had wanted to do a series which used disabled characters as the main characters, but this was seen by the authorities as 'switch-off' time, not entertainment for an audience across the board.

These statements are important for two reasons. First, they establish that some producers do attempt to break the mould, to try something different. Second, and equally important, they show that the efforts of producers are in the final analysis dependent on the approval of those in positions of responsibility. Unless those with power grant their approval and the appropriate resources, the ideas will not develop further.

As one producer put it:

There is a lack of understanding among those people who make decisions about programmes. They do not perceive people with disabilities as an integrated part of life. Their view is that you've got to make them cry, make them laugh, make them do something and let's not get confused by getting people bunged in wheelchairs. 'We have enough on our hands doing what we have to do'. That is the common attitude.

Finally,

Controllers are not unsympathetic but are scared about what ordinary viewers might make of it.

For those producers who wish to challenge the accepted way of doing things, the obstacles lie in the hierarchical organisation of television, its economic structures and its understanding of the sensi- bilities of the audience. But is that the whole picture or only a part of a more complex one?

The limited number of interviews conducted during the course of this research point to a degree of displacement of responsibility on many people's parts. Some producers see the controllers as the stumbling block; others suggest that it is the writers who are not coming up with the ideas, and, in turn, some writers place responsibility on the producers and directors. The following will illustrate these points although the background has to be borne in mind of a highly competitive, costly and complex industrial and cultural environment.

First, the producer's 'tale':

I do not usually tell writers what to write.... You don't say to a writer, 'I am now going to insist that a handicapped person appear

in five out of six episodes of ——'. The writer would say this is rid-
iculous because you are forcing me to engineer stories rather than
letting me find my way there. You can't dictate to a writer ... a
writer can only be pointed in the right direction.

Or,

It is difficult to persuade writers. Writers tend to use their own
stories rather than stories imposed upon them.

For some producers, writers are seen as starting from a common base
of a world inhabited by the 'able-bodied': 'Unless there is a specific
reason for a different starting point, from a base that most people in
our society are white and able-bodied'. This seems a strange comment
when some writers must be disabled and others well able to imagine
any given starting point for their storylines.

Writers, by contrast, emphasise the degree of co-operation and
support which must exist between themselves and their producers if
their ideas are to evolve and develop. Without that co-operation and
support, their ideas are worth little and may never be taken up. This
dependency on hierarchical power is often overlooked – intentionally
or unintentionally – by producers. This is never more so than when a
series or soap has many writers contributing to it. Thus, the writer's
'tale':

There are many writers on *Eastenders* and the final say-so on storylines and characters rests with our producer.

Another writer says:

I am not sure the series [a peak-time police series] has anything to
do with ideas. Whether by accident or design, your [the researcher's]
letter identifies my craft contribution to television as 'script writing'.... If I write a play, I remain, at any rate to my own satisfaction,
a 'writer'. If I write something like [the series], I accept an abroga-
tion, or declension of that term.... To resolve my thoughts, if I
wished to commit them to paper, I would need to write a play, [the
series] hardly calls out the same energies.

On such a production, the writer works to the script editor and
producer; and one would be more easily titled the wordsmith. I
never supposed that they wanted more than what are in effect
Quick Crosswords. They had their brief, and I had mine.

Whether these perceptions of the division of responsibility in television are accurate or not is neither here nor there. The point is this: in the routine production line of television prime-time, there are established patterns of behaviour and a commonly understood notion of what is expected and required. And so long as that remains unchallenged, any change, even in portrayals of minorities, is likely to be only at the fringes.

For more fundamental change, a commitment and a determination are needed that are difficult to sustain. The example of Nina in *Crossroads* keeps coming back to mind for its depth of commitment and its honest intention to use the medium as an educational tool. This applies also to *Brookside* and the development of a character with dyslexia. From the point of view of the informed viewer, what makes the difference between the inadequate and the adequate portrayal 'is the quality and sensitivity of researchers and writers and their willingness to listen rather than have preconceived ideas about the types of programmes they want and the messages which they want to put out'.

Such a commitment does appear to apply to many writers, particularly those who go out of their way to include people with disabilities in their works. And it verges on the educational use of television:

> I wanted to write about someone in a wheelchair. I researched that a bit and found that such characters are always portrayed as weak and helpless or bearing up terribly bravely. I wanted to show someone who was in a wheelchair but was not cliched ... who is tough and aggressive.
>
> I tried to show what it was like to be excluded because of being in a wheelchair. It was partly educational. I wanted to include it without obviously campaigning.

A producer of children's television drama expressed it in this way:

> We wanted to show the normal audience that the lives of people with disabilities were important to them. They are human beings.

Another writer said:

> I wanted to treat the child with a disability as a normal child but at the same time to let the audience see that the child has a disability in the same way as you would approach ethnic or religious differences. Our stories feature children with disabilities, but the emotions they go through could apply to any other child as well. I

don't see any differences; there are some differences but essentially they [the children] go through the same traumas as other children.

For those less socially committed, the issue of the portrayal of people with disabilities is not an overwhelmingly important one. One producer, for example, felt that 'there was no real role for people with disabilities' in his series. Even though he admitted to 'nudging' his directors to do something about it, there appears to have been no perceptible change in the content of the series.

A more elaborate reason for not including people with disabilities in programmes, in this case a soap opera, was provided by Bill Podmore, a producer of *Coronation Street*. Although he admitted that people with disabilities could be included if the storyline required it and if story writers came up with 'credible' characters, the fact that none has appeared to date appears to confirm the feeling that those in charge have 'shied away from the idea'. It is not as if the issue has never previously been raised. As Podmore explained:

> I have had letters from various organisations and societies representing disabled people ... and yet quite a lot of these letters tend to have quite a negativist [sic] effect on your thinking, because you say to yourself, 'well, if I was to do that for that society or whatever, then I should really consider this one as well', and you'd finish up with a programme with a blind person, a deaf person, a person in a wheelchair and so on. You also have to consider that if we did finish up with a handicapped person, then the idea would be to get a real handicapped person to play the part.
> (*Same Difference*, Channel 4, 12/2/89)

This view may be countered by pointing out, as did one producer, that it was not a question of not being able to draw the line but that where the line is presently drawn, it completely excludes people with disabilities.

A not dissimilar view was given by the current producer (at the time of writing) of *Coronation Street*, who argued that the programme is primarily a fictional one and so does not derive 'its stories from issues'.[1] To alter that approach for the sake of a particular issue, any issue, would thus appear to be contrary to the spirit of the series.

This is not the place to delve into the relationship between fiction and reality in television, nor to explore the extent to which a programme's success derives from its purchase on reality rather than its evasion of real situations. What is interesting about this correspondence, as well as Podmore's earlier statement, is the perception of disability as an issue, not as a fact of life.

To see it as an issue is to misunderstand the nature of the debate which is now being conducted. People with disabilities wish to be seen on television because they are part of life and not alien to it. They do not want to use the box as a soap box but as a 'window on the world' in which they exist. But as long as television treats people with disabilities as an issue – is the demand for the representation of a multifaceted, multicultural society an issue? – it will continue to ignore a very fundamental demand of people with disabilities to become visible and enter the public's consciousness.

The achievement of integration is one that more 'positive' imagery alone is unlikely to win single-handedly. Other major social changes would have to take place to accompany the desire to achieve that aim; and such changes would need to include the provision of access to all facets of life, something that will happen only, in the view of many discussants, when people with disabilities are asked about their attitudes, feelings and needs and are not just given what others think they need.

Conclusions

1 People with disabilities do appear in factual programmes broadcast over British television. In the period examined people with disabilities appeared in 16 per cent of all the factual programmes analysed but this proportion rose to 24 per cent of news programmes. They did not appear at all in current affairs programmes during the period examined. Not one of the 44 game shows observed contained a single person with a disability.

2 There was some variation between channels in the amount of broadcasting which included people with disabilities, BBC1 and ITV showing more people with disabilities than either Channel 4 or BBC2. This variation would appear to be due to the fact that BBC2 does not show news programmes and Channel 4 does not show regional news. It is in regional rather than national news items that people with disabilities are most likely to appear.

3 The most common focus for factual reporting that involved people with disabilities was that of medical treatment. This was the theme in 16 per cent of the cases examined. In 11 per cent the focus was upon the special achievement of the disabled person and in 9 per cent it was on the cure for the particular disability displayed. The emphasis on medical treatment was even greater when news programmes alone were examined; here medical treatment represented 22 per cent of all cases mentioned. In contrast, what we have called 'other factual programmes' (that is, those programmes not easily defined) focused most commonly upon the special achievement of people with disabilities. This theme constituted 25 per cent of the themes of such programmes.

4 The tone of these factual programmes concerning people with disabilities is not always easy to categorise, and it might seem churlish to comment upon the fact that many of the commentators put the emphasis on sympathy for people with disabilities and congratulations to them on their 'special' achievements. However, it cannot always be appropriate to adopt a tone that emphasises the misfortunes of people with disabilities and their courage in overcoming them; this is to cloak the presentation in the garb of sentimentality and is often found to be offensive by those with disabilities and at least inappropriate by other viewers. The objection to this style of presentation is that by inducing sympathy the feelings of concern aroused in the audience are simply dissipated. The issue, which could be raised and discussed and acted upon, is thereby simply swept away.

5 People with disabilities were portrayed in fictional programmes but they represented a mere 0.5 per cent of all the characters portrayed. When only major and minor (that is, speaking) characters are considered, the percentage rises to 1.4 per cent. This contrasts strangely with the evidence of the Office of Population Censuses and Surveys that 14 per cent of the adult population of Britain has disabilities of one kind or another. However, the population portrayed on television is not at all the same as the UK population. For example, the television population displayed in the 6 weeks of our content analysis proved to be 65 per cent male, 95 per cent white and over 50 per cent between the ages of 25 and 40. When allowance is made for the peculiar structure of the television population, it would then appear that 6.81 per cent of the characters presented should be shown as disabled, in contrast to the 0.5 per cent of characters in dramatic fiction programmes actually portrayed to have disabilities.

6 The characters depicted as having some disability or other are overwhelmingly shown to have locomotor, behavioural or disfigurement disabilities. Presumably, this is because such disabilities are so obviously visible. The wheelchair has apparently become a ready symbol of the experience of disability, a shorthand for a variety of difficulties that someone suffering from disabilities may encounter. We must, however, remark that the range of disabilities portrayed is conspicuously narrow, even if we understand that the reason for this is that certain disabilities are much more easily

portrayed than others. It is not so much the real world that is being portrayed as the readily screenable world.

7 Among fictional programmes it is worth commenting that only 8 per cent of soap opera episodes contained someone with a disability and only 9 per cent of episodes of situation comedies. The genres in which people with disabilities were most likely to have been seen during the viewing period were crime and thriller films.

8 In contrast to drama programmes, feature films are more than twice as likely to include disabled characters. In our analysis 134 films were examined and 72 proved to contain disabled characters. Of these, 53 included people with disabilities in major or minor speaking parts, and of these 53 films, 25 made the circumstance of disability an important issue.

9 The way in which the issue was treated in feature films varied, and in more than half of the cases (13) it was judged to be purely sentimental. In only 8 of these films was the issue of prejudice and discrimination against people with disabilities and the need for them to establish their rights the issue chosen for emphasis.

10 We have concluded that the portrayal of characters with disabilities in feature films tends to be through stereotypes, and that the most commonly used stereotypes are the disabled person as a criminal or only barely human or someone who is powerless and pathetic. The stereotype of the disabled person as a criminal occurred in 6 of the 72 films examined; that of the subhuman occurred in 5 of these films and that of the pathetic person in 7. The overall conclusion is that characters with disabilities are included in the storylines of feature films for ulterior motives: that is, not because they are ordinary people whom one might expect to encounter in an ordinary society, to the contrary, they would appear to be brought in to enhance the atmosphere of a film when it needs to be one of deprivation or mystery or menace. In short, disabled characters are introduced not because they are ordinary people like others but in order to suggest precisely the opposite, that they are not ordinary people.

11 When the portrayal of disabled characters is compared and contrasted with the portrayal of able-bodied characters, it is immediately apparent that the disabled characters are of lower

status. They are less likely to be in professional or white-collar employment (6 per cent:20 per cent) and more likely to be unemployed (12 per cent:5 per cent) and over 60 (17 per cent:4.6 per cent). They are evidently low status people whose status is yet further lowered by their disabilities.

12 The attitudes displayed towards disabled characters are also markedly different to those shown toward able-bodied characters. Disabled characters are much more likely to evoke sympathy (34 per cent:7 per cent), pity (12 per cent:2 per cent), sadness (16 per cent:3 per cent), fear (16 per cent:7 per cent) or a patronising attitude (30 per cent:14 per cent). In contrast, able-bodied characters are much more likely to evoke respect (51 per cent:39 per cent) or attraction (43 per cent:33 per cent). The lowly character of the disabled is lowered again through the attitudes and behaviour of the able-bodied.

13 In terms of the relationships portrayed, disabled characters were less likely to be involved in sexual relationships with other characters (12 per cent:22 per cent) and more likely to be 'loners' (35 per cent:25 per cent).

14 Characters with disabilities are portrayed even more negatively than we have so far suggested. We have already noted that they are much more likely than able-bodied characters to be portrayed as villains. However, they are also more likely to be portrayed as 'difficult to get on with', moody, introverted, unsociable or sad. Further, disabled characters were far more likely than their able-bodied compatriots to be either aggressive or the victims of violence; and they were more than three times as likely as able-bodied characters to be dead by the end of the programme. We must also remark that the fate of these disabled characters was invariably treated as a personal and individual matter (thus their deaths were regularly depicted as being the result of their disabilities). Seldom was any suggestion made in these films that society or social arrangements or social attitudes and values had any bearing upon the fate of these people.

15 When the portrayal of disabled people in British dramatic fictional programmes is compared and contrasted with the portrayal of such characters in programmes from the US, it is found that disabled characters in US programmes are more likely

than their UK counterparts to be sociable, extrovert, moral and non-aggressive and less likely to be dependent, sad, moody or difficult to get on with. The attitudes evoked by the US disabled characters are also more respectful and unaggressive than is the case in UK productions. Disabled characters in US productions were much more likely to have an emotional relationship (63 per cent) than were such characters in UK productions (26 per cent), although those in UK productions were less likely than their US counterparts to have no relationships at all (12 per cent:23 per cent).

16 In our discussion groups the definition of disabled people or people with disabilities was an issue of first importance. Most people would appear to see people with disabilities as in a medical category, although they are becoming increasingly aware of the social dimension of the definition of people as having disabilities, even if this is not yet as widespread as those who press for a better understanding of the experience of disability would wish to see. Many more people implicitly recognise that society and able-bodied people have a hand in 'disabling' people with disabilities than express this idea openly. We must recognise that among disabled people the social construction of disability is frequently taken for granted, and a more 'extreme' position is embraced in which 'disability' is seen not just as a social but as a political category. Such a definition brings disabled people into line with those black people, women, gay people and other representatives of minorities who are not receiving their due in British society and who are contending for their social and political rights.

17 Our survey of the general public brought out the fact that it is widely recognised that people with disabilities are under-portrayed in different types of television genre. Even though members of the public do not know what proportion of the population as a whole is disabled, they none the less recognise that this part of the population is underrepresented on the television screen. The public does not believe that there are too many drama programmes on television which feature people with disabilities and it does believe that there are too few such programmes. Further, the majority (71 per cent) believe that people with disabilities should appear in all types of programmes and there is little belief that people with disabilities should be restricted to

their own programmes; more than 80 per cent of those surveyed did not believe this.

18 A strong majority (74 per cent) of the sample surveyed disagreed with the suggestion that they sometimes felt embarrassed at seeing severely disabled people on television. Of course, the converse of this is that 26 per cent did not disagree with the idea that they get embarrassed in this context, and naturally that minority opinion has to be respected. In like manner, a minority of 37 per cent felt that some disabilities were 'too disturbing and should not be shown on television'. Interestingly, disabled respondents were slightly more likely to feel embarrassed or disturbed by the appearance of people with disabilities than were able-bodied respondents.

19 The issue of whether actors with disabilities should be employed to play disabled characters is not simple. In the case of some severe disabilities it may be that someone actually suffering from them would not be able to perform the part of someone required to exhibit those disabilities dramatically. Occasionally also someone with a real disability playing the part of a character with that disability may have the effect of destroying the convention of pretence that theatrical performances assume. There are three possible policy initiatives which should be considered here: the development of training of disabled actors; an affirmative action programme, that is, casting disabled performers in roles for which their disability is not 'a need'; or seeking of every opportunity for disabled performers to play the parts of characters with disabilities.

20 If there are to be more disabled characters portrayed on television then writers and producers have to accept responsibility for providing such parts. At least there is now debate about how this could be achieved. There is some reluctance to write a part for a disabled character in a television series, but if this is not done, then the appearances of disabled characters will inevitably be few and far between. There do need to be series written and produced in which people with disabilities are among the leading characters. Should this occur, then the public would be regularly confronted with the experience of disability in a perfectly ordinary context. The most ordinary context is presumably that of the realistic soap opera and we strongly urge writers and producers of soap operas to accept the continuing challenge to provide such roles. There are

a number of complex questions raised by this suggestion, but little reason why they should not be tackled honestly and with determination.

21 We recognise and acclaim a number of instances in which this has occurred and been tackled with honesty and commitment. We therefore urge the management of production companies also to accept the challenge and provide the opportunities for it to be met.

22 We thus return to the point at which we began. Given that people with disabilities wish to be treated first and foremost as people, and only secondarily as people who happen to have disabilities, they should be so treated on television. In factual programmes this means that producers must be on their guard that people with disabilities are not used in a sentimental manner, to give to able-bodied viewers a sense of the superiority of their condition or the emotional enjoyment of their generous sympathy. People with disabilities are like able-bodied people: sometimes brave, sometimes not brave, sometimes fortunate, sometimes unfortunate, sometimes enjoying success and sometimes not doing so. This is the way in which they should be portrayed. In fictional programmes equally people with disabilities should be represented as a part of ordinary life and not alien to it. They should be part of the drama of life as presented on television, and not used in either a sinister or sentimental manner.

23 To ask for this consideration for people with disabilities is to ask of the television world first that it should reflect the real world more faithfully than it habitually does, by not concealing the existence of people with disabilities in society, and second that it should act as a force for the improvement of that real world in which, unfortunately, people with disabilities have yet to secure the rights and privileges which a society that espouses liberal and democratic values should make every endeavour to accord them.

24 Our society should invite people with disabilities to express their own attitudes, feelings and needs, and then listen to them and honestly hear them. Should this occur, people with disabilities may be given what they need rather than what others think they need; and this could apply to television as well as to other areas of life.

Appendix I
Office of Population, Censuses and Surveys coding guide

TYPES OF DISABILITY – INDEX

I. LOCOMOTION

Severity score

11.5	1.	Cannot walk at all
9.5	2.	Can only walk a few steps without severe discomfort/ cannot walk up and down one step
7.5	3.	Falls over
7.0	4.	Always needs to hold onto something to keep balance
6.5	5.	Cannot walk up and down a flight of stairs
5.5	6.	Cannot walk 50 yards without stopping or severe discomfort

4.5	7. Cannot bend down far enough to pick something up from the floor and straighten up again
3.0	9. Cannot walk 200 yards without severe discomfort or stopping/can only walk up a flight of stairs if holds on and takes a rest/often needs to hold on to something to keep balance
2.5	10. Can only walk up a flight of stairs if holds on (doesn't need a rest)
2.0	11. Cannot bend down to sweep something up from the floor and straighten up again
1.5	13. Cannot walk 400 yards without stopping or severe discomfort
0.0	14. Lame (club foot, calipers, bad limp, etc.)

II. REACHING AND STRETCHING

9.5	15. Cannot hold out either arm in front to shake hands
9.0	16. Cannot put either arm up to head to put on a hat
8.0	17. Cannot put either hand behind to put on jacket or tuck in shirt
7.0	18. Cannot raise either arm above head to reach for something
6.5	19. Has difficulty holding either arm in front to shake hands
5.5	20. Has difficulty putting either arm up to head
4.5	21. Has difficulty putting either hand behind back
3.5	22. Has difficulty raising either arm above head
2.5	23. Cannot hold one arm out to front or up to head (but can with other)
1.0	24. Cannot or has difficulty putting one arm behind back (but can use other one)/cannot or has difficulty putting one arm out in front or up to head (but no difficulty with other arm)

III. DEXTERITY

10.5	25. Cannot pick up and hold a mug with either hand
9.5	26. Cannot turn on a tap with either hand
8.0	27. Cannot pick up a pint of milk or squeeze water from a sponge with either hand

7.0	28. Cannot pick up a small object with either hand
6.5	29. Has difficulty picking up and pouring from a full kettle or serving food from a pan using a spoon or ladle
5.5	30. Has difficulty unscrewing the lid of a coffee jar or writing with a pen or pencil
4.0	31. Cannot pick up and carry a 5lb bag of potatoes
3.0	32. Has difficulty wringing out light washing or using a pair of scissors
2.0	33. Can pick up and hold a mug with one hand but not the other
1.5	34. Can turn on a tap or squeeze water from a sponge with one hand but not the other
0.5	35. Can pick up a small object with one hand but not the other/has difficulty tying a bow in laces

IV. PERSONAL CARE

11.0	36. Cannot feed self without help/cannot go to and use the toilet without help
9.5	37. Cannot get into and out of bed or a chair without help
7.0	38. Cannot wash hands or face without help/cannot dress and undress without help
4.5	39. Cannot wash all over without help
2.5	40. Has difficulty feeding self/has difficulty getting to and from the toilet without help
1.0	41. Has difficulty getting in and out of bed or chair

V. CONTINENCE

11.5	42. No voluntary control over bowels
10.5	43. No voluntary control over bladder
10.0	44. Loses control over bowels at least once a day
8.0	45. Loses control over bladder at least once a day
8.0	46. Loses control of bowels at least once a week
5.5	47. Loses control of bladder at least once a week
3.0	48. Loses control of bowels or bladder occasionally
1.0	49. Uses a device to control bowels or bladder

VI. SEEING

12.0	50. Cannot tell by the light where the windows are
11.0	51. Cannot see shape of furniture in a room
10.0	52. Cannot recognise a friend if close to his face
8.0	53. Cannot recognise a friend at arm's length
5.5	54. Cannot read a newspaper headline
5.0	55. Cannot read a large print book
4.5	56. Cannot recognise a friend across a room
1.5	57. Cannot recognise a friend across a road
0.5	58. Has difficulty reading ordinary newsprint

VII. HEARING

11.0	59. Cannot hear sounds at all
8.5	60. Cannot follow a TV programme with the sound turned up
6.0	61. Has difficulty hearing someone speaking loud in a quiet room
5.5	62. Cannot hear a doorbell, alarm, telephone, etc.
5.0	63. Cannot use the telephone
4.5	64. Cannot follow a TV programme at a normal volume
1.5	65. Difficulty hearing a normal voice in a quiet room
0.5	66. Difficulty hearing a conversation against a background noise

VIII. COMMUNICATION

12.0	67. Is impossible for people who know him/her well to understand/finds it impossible to understand people who know him/her well
8.5	68. Is impossible for strangers to understand/is very difficult for people who know him/her well to understand/finds it impossible to understand strangers/finds it very difficult to understand people who know him/her well
5.5	69. Is very difficult for strangers to understand/is quite difficult for people who know him/her well to understand/finds it difficult to understand strangers/finds it quite difficult to understand people s/he knows

2.0   70. Is quite difficult for strangers to understand/finds it quite difficult to understand strangers

1.0   71. Other people have some difficulty understanding/has some difficulty understanding what other people say/mean

IX. BEHAVIOUR

10.0   72. Gets so upset that hits other people or injures self

7.5   73. Gets so upset that breaks or rips things up

7.0   74. Feels the need to have someone present all the time

6.0   75. Finds relationships with the family difficult

4.0   76. Often has outbursts of temper with little cause

2.5   77. Finds relationships outside the family very difficult

1.5   78. Sometimes sits for hours doing nothing

0.5   79. Finds it difficult to stir him/herself to do things/often feels aggressive or hostile towards other people

X. INTELLECTUAL FUNCTIONING

13.0   80. Often forgets what supposed to be doing in middle of something

12.0   81. Often loses track of what is being said in mid conversation

10.5   82. Thoughts tend to be muddled or slow

9.5   83. Confused about time of day

8.0   84. Cannot watch TV and tell someone about it

7.0   85. Cannot remember and pass on a message correctly

6.0   86. Often forgets to turn things off such as fires, cookers, taps, etc.

4.5   87. Often forgets names of family and close friends

3.5   88. Cannot read a short article in a newspaper

2.0   89. Cannot write a short letter to someone without help

1.0   90. Cannot count well enough to handle money

XI. CONSCIOUSNESS

Score			Add scores for following items	
12.0	13.8	91.	Has fits:	
11.5	12.8–13	92.	Once but less than 4 times a year	1
10.5	11.8	93.	4 times but less than monthly	2
10.0	10.8	94.	Monthly but less than weekly	3
9.0	9.8–10	95.	Weekly but less than daily	4
8.0	8.8–9	96.	Every day	5
7.0	7.8–8	97.	Only during night	1
6.0	6.8–7	98.	At night or on waking	3.8
5.0	5.8–6	99.	At night, on waking, in evening	5.8
4.0	4.8–5	100.	During the day	3.8
3.0	4.0	101.	Always has warning before	1
2.0	3.0	102.	Has fit without warning	0
1.0	2.0	103.	Loses consciousness during fit	1
0.5	1.0	104.	Does not lose consciousness	0

XII. EATING, DRINKING AND DIGESTING

0.5	105.	Suffers problems with eating, drinking or digestion which severely affects ability to lead normal life

XIII. DISFIGUREMENT

0.5	106.	Dwarfism
0.5	107.	Suffers from a scar, blemish or deformity which affects ability to lead a normal life

XIV. OTHERS

0	108.	Suffers from diabetes

Appendix II
Coding schedule

TYPES OF DISABILITY – GENERAL

1. Blind
2. Partially sighted
3.
4.
5. Deaf
6. Partially deaf
7.
8.
9. One missing limb
10. More than one missing limb
11. Malformed limb/s
12. Seriously disfigured body
13. Slightly disfigured body
14. Seriously disfigured face
15. Slightly disfigured face
16.
17.
18.
19. Cerebral palsy, wheelchair bound
20. Cerebral palsy, walking with aid
21. Cerebral palsy, walking without aid
22.
23.
24. Partial paralysis
25. Cannot walk
26. Complete paralysis
27. Lame

28.
29.
30.   Mute, cannot speak
31.   Speech defect
32.
33.   Spina Bifida
34.   Hydrocephalus
35.
36.   Disfiguring disease (e.g. psoriasis)
37.
38.   Dwarfism
39.
40.
41.   Down's Syndrome
42.
43.   Mentally ill (dependent, cannot live alone)
44.   Mentally ill (independent, sporadic effects)
45.
46.
47.   Mentally handicapped, serious (no/few living skills)
48.   Mentally handicapped, moderate (not independent)
49.   Mentally handicapped (slow learner)
50.   Brain damage, severe (dependent)
51.   Brain damage (independent)
52.
53.   Disorientation
54.
55.

CODING SCHEDULE

Programme sheet

       Programme title ....
1.   Programme number ....
2.   Channel   BBC1 = 1   BBC2 = 2   ITV = 3   Channel 4 = 4
3.   Date of transmission ....
4.   Coding date ....
5.   Start time (24 hour clock) ....
6.   Video counter start ....

7.   Video counter end ....

8.   Genre (see separate sheet) ....

9.   Country of production
      0. Cannot code   1. U.K.   2. U.S.   3. Australia   4. Europe
      5. Other

10.   Production type
      0. Cannot code
      1. Factual (news, documentaries, etc.)
      2. Feature film (made for cinema)
      3. Film, made for television
      4. Part of drama series (including soap opera and sitcoms)
      5. Other dramatic
      6. Other

11.   Running time (minutes) ....

12.   Coder ....

13.   Disability portrayed
      0. Cannot code (explain)   1. Yes   2. No

14.   Disability not portrayed but discussed
      0. Cannot code (explain)   1. Yes (fill in discussion about
      disability section)

15.   Total number of characters
      With disability
                        Major ....
                        Minor ....
                        Incidental ....
                        Background ....
      Without disability
                        Major ....
                        Minor ....
                        Incidental ....
                        Background ....

16.   If any incidental or background disabled characters
      appeared were they
         0. Cannot code
         1. Part of general public, normal bystanders
         2. Used as a spectacle, out of the ordinary

17.   Location of incidental and background disabled characters
         0. Cannot code/none
         1. Institution
         2. Domestic

            3. Public setting
            4. Other
18.   Estimated year of production (drama only) . . . .
19.   Was there sex or violence? (note counter numbers and
        prefix with code 1–4)
            1. Sex shown
            2. Sex implied
            3. Much violence
            4. A little violence
            5. Cannot code

Character profile

            Programme title . . . .
1.   Programme code . . . .
2.   Character number . . . .
3.   Genre and country . . . .
4.   Level of appearance
            0. Cannot code
            1. Major
            2. Minor
5.   Centrality to plot
            0. Cannot code
            1. Central
            2. Not central
6.   Is the character
            0. Cannot code
            1. Physically disabled
            2. Mentally ill
            3. Mentally handicapped
            4. Both physically disabled and mentally ill
            5. Both physically disabled and mentally handicapped
            6. Sensory disability
            7. Other
            8. Non-disabled
7.   Age (leave blank if cannot code and explain)
8.   Ethnic origin
            0. Cannot code
            1. White
            2. Black
            3. Asian/oriental

4. Other
9. Sex
0. Cannot code   1. Male   2. Female
10. Profession
0. Cannot code
1. Professional
2. White-collar
3. Blue-collar
4. Unemployed
5. Housewife
6. Nurse, doctor, care professional
7. Public service professional
8. Other
11. Financial status
0. Cannot code
1. Rich
2. Wealthy
3. Comfortable
4. Subsisting
5. Poor
6. Destitute
12. Marital status
0. Cannot code
1. Single
2. Co-habiting
3. Married
4. Single with children
5. Co-habiting with children
6. Married with children
7. Separated
13. Character type
0. Cannot code
1. Basically good
2. Neutral, neither good nor bad, mixed
3. Basically bad
14. Personality traits (code only when trait is an obvious part of the character's personality, otherwise leave blank)
1. Sociable   1 2 3 4 5 Unsociable
2. Extrovert   1 2 3 4 5 Introvert
3. Independent   1 2 3 4 5 Dependent

4. Aware/worldly		1	2	3	4	5	Naive
5. Happy	1	2	3	4	5	Sad
6. Carefree	1	2	3	4	5	Moody
7. Amiable	1	2	3	4	5	Difficult
8. Liked	1	2	3	4	5	Disliked
9. Socially accepted		1	2	3	4	5	Socially unaccepted
10. Moral	1	2	3	4	5	Immoral
11. Non-aggressive	1	2	3	4	5	Aggressive

15. Nature in which the character is portrayed (code most obvious/relevant attribute)
   0. Cannot code
   1. Hero
   2. Anti-hero (a hero but in the eyes of the law a villain)
   3. Villain
   4. Victim
   5. Subhuman/monster
   6. Neutral
   7. Other
16. Sexuality of character
   0. Cannot code
   1. Heterosexual
   2. Homosexual
   3. Bisexual
   4. Asexual
   5. Deviant
   6. Mixed
17. Attitudes shown towards character (code all that apply)
   0. Cannot code
   1. Treated as any person
   2. Sympathy
   3. Attraction
   4. Fear
   5. Abuse
   6. Pity
   7. Mocking
   8. Avoidance
   9. Patronising
   10. Respect
   11. Aggression

12. Sadness
13. None of above

18.   Is the character portrayed as
    0. Cannot code
    1. A loner
    2. Mixing mainly with the disabled
    3. Mixing mainly with disabled and able-bodied
    4. Mixing with able-bodied only?

19.   Is the character portrayed as doing something
    useful/constructive, achieving something?
    Yes, very   1 2 3 4 5 No, not at all
    0. Cannot code

20.   Relationships: Does the character have (code more than
    one if necessary)
    0. Cannot code
    1. Emotional relationships (excluding sibling and
        professional)
    2. Sexual relationships (shown or implied)
    3. Family relationships (sibling, parent, spouse, etc.)
    4. Potential emotional or sexual relationship
    5. None

21.   Social status
    0. Cannot code
    1. Highly respected
    2. Normal/average/neutral
    3. Low

22.   Is the character treated as a lesser person?
    0. Cannot code
    1. Always
    2. Sometimes
    3. Never

23.   Group status
    0. Cannot code
    1. Not an obvious member of a group
    2. Respected member of a group
    3. Normal/average/neutral
    4. Low status

24.   Mode of dress – how does it compare to the majority of
    other characters in the programme?
    0. Cannot code

1. Similar (as fashionable, tidy, etc.)
2. Less fashionable than most
3. Untidier, scruffier than most
4. More eccentric (wearing odd clothes knowingly)
5. More fashionable than most
6. Smarter than most

25.   Is the character portrayed as being odd, mysterious or eccentric?
   0. Cannot code
   1. Extremely
   2. Fairly
   3. Not at all

26.   Does the character bear any resentment towards other characters or society as a whole?
   0. Cannot code
   1. Yes, to other characters
   2. Yes, to society
   3. Yes, to both
   4. None

27.   Does the character display any of the following types of attitudes towards disabled characters in the programme?
   0. Cannot code
   1. Treated as any person
   2. Sympathy
   3. Attraction
   4. Fear
   5. Abuse
   6. Pity
   7. Mocking
   8. Avoidance
   9. Patronising
   10. Respect
   11. Aggression
   12. Sadness
   13. None of above

28.   Eventual outcome of the character
   0. Cannot code
   1. Positive/happy
   2. Neutral
   3. Negative/unhappy

4. Death
5. Suicide
6. Other

29. Is the character involved in violence? (code all that apply)
    0. Cannot code
    1. Yes, as aggressor
    2. As a witness
    3. As a victim
    4. No

30. If violence is used is it
    0. Cannot code
    1. Provoked (include self-defence and war)
    2. Unprovoked
    3. Both

31. Is criminality connected to the character, in real terms or mentioned?
    0. Cannot code
    1. Real terms, i.e. is a criminal
    2. Is criminally insane
    3. Suggested, i.e. is called criminally insane
    4. No

32. Is the character portrayed as being dangerous to others?
    0. Cannot code
    1. Always
    2. Sometimes
    3. Never

33. Is the character likely to be respected by the audience?
    Completely   1 2 3 4 5 Not at all
    0. Cannot code

34. Did the character wear glasses?
    0. Cannot code
    1. Always
    2. Sometimes
    3. Never
    (make a note of any relevant counter numbers)

35. Estimated year of production ....

Code for disabled characters only

    Programme title . . . .
1. Programme code . . . .
2. Character number and name of character . . . .
3. Genre and country . . . .
4. Type of disability (see separate sheet)(code up to 3 categories)
5. Type of disability general (see separate sheet)
                                        (code up to 2 categories)
6. Type of aids used (see separate sheet)
7. Is the disability age-related?
    0. Cannot code   1. Yes   2. No
8. Is the disability temporary?
    0. Cannot code   1. Yes   2. No
9. Does the disability occur during the programme?
    0. Cannot code   1. Yes   2. No
10. Are the physical or mental attributes of the character used
    to shock or scare either other characters or the audience?
    0. Cannot code   1. Yes   2. No
11. Is the character's disability exploited by able-bodied
    characters, e.g. Elephant man, terrorising blind people?
    0. Cannot code
    1. Never
    2. Once/occasionally
    3. Several times
    4. Frequently
12. Are any of the physical difficulties of being disabled shown?
    0. Cannot code
    1. Much of the time
    2. Occasionally
    3. Not at all
13. Is any prejudice/negative discrimination directed against
    the disabled character?
    0. Cannot code
    1. Much of the time
    2. Occasionally
    3. Not at all
14. If a disabled person appeared were any of the following
    part of the storyline relating to the character?
    (code up to 3 categories)
    0. Cannot code

1. Achievement (special)
2. Achievement (fitting into 'normal life')
3. Prejudice/discrimination
4. Tragedy
5. Victim
6. Treatment/cure
7. Rehabilitation
8. None of the above (specify)

15.   Are the disabled characters passive or do they speak out against individuals or society mistreating/patronising them?
0. Cannot code
1. Passive
2. Against individuals only
3. Against society only
4. Against both individuals and society

16.   Are the complaints put forward by individuals not as part of a group or is there some form of organisation behind the protest? (e.g. in most productions which deal with rights for ethnic minorities they are shown to be organised into groups and not fighting from individual standpoints)
0. Cannot code
1. Individual
2. Group unofficial/informal
3. Group official/formal

17.   Is the portrayal used explicitly or implicitly (e.g. through parody) to highlight the problems of being disabled with regard to other people's attitudes or society's failure to recognise special needs (e.g. lack of ramps or obstacles on pavements)?
0. Cannot code
1. No
2. Individual's failure to recognise special needs
3. Society's failure to recognise special needs
4. Both

18.   Is the character content or discontented?
0. Cannot code
1. Content
2. Discontented
3. Mixture
If content, why: ....

FILL IN ON ANSWER SHEET

19. Does the character appear discontented because s/he cannot do the things that able-bodied people can do or that s/he used to be able to do?
    0. Cannot code
    1. Extremely
    2. Fairly/sometimes
    3. Not at all

20. Does the character appear dissatisfied with the way in which individuals treat/interact with him/her?
    0. Cannot code
    1. Extremely
    2. Fairly/sometimes
    3. Not at all

21. Does the character appear discontented with the way in which s/he is treated by society in general/people in general?
    0. Cannot code
    1. Extremely
    2. Fairly/sometimes
    3. Not at all

22. Does the character appear to be preoccupied with his/her disability?
    0. Cannot code
    1. Very preoccupied
    2. Fairly
    3. Not at all

23. Is the character perceived by him/herself to be inferior to those without a disability?
    0. Cannot code
    1. Always
    2. Sometimes
    3. Never

24. Is the feeling of inferiority a reflection of self-esteem or is the feeling only prompted by outside experiences?
    0. Cannot code
    1. Low self-esteem
    2. Negative outside experiences
    3. Mixture

25. Is there any mention of a movement for disability rights or the need for such a movement (either stated or implied)?

       0. Cannot code
       1. Yes
       2. No
26.   Does there appear to be a metaphorical message tied in with the characterisation?
       0. Cannot code
       1. Yes
       2. No
       (If the answer is yes, describe in what manner on the synopsis sheet under the heading METAPHOR.)
27.   Is the disabled character looked after by able-bodied character/s? (include hospitalised characters)
       0. Cannot code
       1. Always
       2. Sometimes
       3. Not at all
28.   Do the disabled characters have power and freedom of movement taken away by able-bodied characters?
       0. Cannot code
       1. Always
       2. Sometimes/to a certain extent
       3. Not at all
29.   Does the character have power and freedom of choice/ movement taken away by other circumstances (e.g. bed-bound)?
       0. Cannot code
       1. Always
       2. Sometimes/to a certain extent
       3. Not at all
30.   Does the character look physically like an able-bodied person?
       0. Cannot code
       1. Yes
       2. No
31.   Is the character talked to through a third party?
       0. Cannot code
       1. Always
       2. Sometimes
       3. Never
32.   Is the character treated in a childlike manner?

0. Cannot code
1. Always
2. Sometimes
3. Never
33. Is the character cured?
0. Cannot code
1. Yes, by unexplained/supernatural/religious means
2. Yes, by medical means
3. Yes, by the will to be cured
4. No
34. Is there any mention/suggestion/implication that willpower,
     self confidence and the 'belief that you can/will recover'
     may directly lead to or help in a cure/improvement?
0. Cannot code
1. Briefly/vaguely
2. Strong suggestion
3. Not at all
35. Is the fact that the character is disabled seen as a tragedy?
0. Cannot code
1. By all of the characters
2. By some of the characters
3. Just by the disabled character
4. By other characters but not by the disabled character
5. Not at all
36. Is the character worried about how the disability may affect
     them (e.g. they may have a fit)?
0. Cannot code
1. Yes
2. No
37. Can the disabled character communicate effectively (can
     s/he talk, sign – not cut off from the world)?
0. Cannot code
1. Yes
2. Partially/sometimes
3. Not at all
38. Does the portrayal suggest that the character should strive
     for a cure and would be better off/happier for it?
0. Cannot code
1. Yes
2. Partially/sometimes

3. Not at all
39. Main location of character
    0. Cannot code
    1. Institution for the disabled (hospital, home, etc.)
    2. Other
    3. Mixed
40. Is criminality connected to the characterisation (either in actual terms, i.e. s/he is a criminal or in suggested terms, i.e. called criminally insane, kept under lock and key/ guarded in an institution)?
    0. Cannot code
    1. Real terms, i.e. is a criminal
    2. Criminally insane
    3. Suggested, e.g. called criminally insane
    4. No
41. Is the character portrayed as being dangerous?
    0. Cannot code
    1. Always
    2. Sometimes
    3. Never
42. Estimated year of production ....

Factual programmes

Programme title ....
1. Programme code ....
2. Genre
   1. News
   2. Documentary
   3. Current affairs
   4. Magazine
3. Number of items in the programme ....
4. Number of items referring to disabled people ....
5. People involved
   0. Cannot code
   1. One disabled person
   2. Group disabled people
   3. Mixed group
   4. Disabled people and care auxiliary/professional
6. Age group of disabled people
   0. Cannot code

   1. Children (under 13)
   2. Adolescents
   3. Children and adolescents
   4. Adults (over 18)
   5. Mixed
7. Types of disability shown (from general disability sheet)
8. Type of story (code up to 3 categories)
   0. Cannot code
   1. Achievement (special)
   2. Achievement (fitting into 'normal life')
   3. Rehabilitation
   4. Cure (explanation of a type of cure)
   5. Treatment/therapy
   6. Prejudice
   7. Tragedy
   8. Victim
   9. Struggle for equality
   10. Mixed
   11. Other (specify)
9. Were the disabled people the main focus of the story?
   0. Cannot code
   1. Yes
   2. No
   3. Unsure
   (Do disabled people ever appear in stories that are not
   specifically about disability?)
10. Were the presenters disabled?
   0. Cannot code
   1. Yes/all of them
   2. Some of them
   3. No/none of them
11. Language used by presenters
   0. Cannot code
   1. Neutral (disabled person, no mention of disability)
   2. Impersonal (the disabled, the handicapped, etc.)
   3. Slang, derogatory terms (cripples, mongols, etc.)
   4. Mixed
   5. Other
   (See separate sheet for examples)
   Phrase used: ....

12. Would the item have been included/the programme made
    if the subjects had not been disabled?
    0. Cannot code
    1. Yes
    2. No
13. Do able-bodied people interpret or add to statements made
    by disabled people?
    0. Cannot code
    1. All of the time/often
    2. Sometimes
    3. Not at all
14. Were adjectives such as 'brave', 'plucky', 'courageous'
    used to describe the disabled person?
    0. Cannot code
    1. Often
    2. Sometimes
    3. Never
15. Were adjectives such as 'unfortunate', 'unhappy' or phrases
    such as 'little to smile about', 'fighting adversity', etc. used?
    0. Cannot code
    1. Yes, often
    2. Sometimes
    3. No
16. Were the physical difficulties or general coping difficulties
    of being disabled discussed?
    0. Cannot code
    1. Not at all
    2. Briefly/vaguely
    3. In some depth
17. Did the story/programme dwell on fitting into normal life/
    being able to do everyday things?
    0. Cannot code
    1. Not at all
    2. Briefly/vaguely
    3. In some depth
18. Did the story dwell on the finding of a cure/explanation or a
    cure/therapy?
    0. Cannot code
    1. Not at all

2. Briefly/vaguely
3. In some depth

19. Did the story dwell on the experiences of one person or a group of people undergoing treatment/therapy?
   0. Cannot code
   1. Not at all
   2. Briefly/vaguely
   3. In some depth

20. Were the problems disabled people face due to the lack of understanding, concern, etc. of able-bodied people/society discussed?
   0. Cannot code
   1. Not at all
   2. Briefly/vaguely
   3. In some depth

21. Does the report acknowledge the fact that disabled people have rights to fight for?
   0. Cannot code
   1. Not at all
   2. Briefly/vaguely
   3. In some depth

22. Main location of the report
   0. Cannot code
   1. Institution for the disabled (hospital, home, etc.)
   2. Other
   3. Mixed

23. Does it come over in the story that the disabled person/s would rather be able-bodied?
   0. Cannot code
   1. Strongly
   2. To a certain extent
   3. Not at all

24. Do the disabled people speak during the item/programme?
   0. Cannot code
   1. For much of the time
   2. Briefly
   3. One or two words
   4. Not at all

SUMMARY OF THE NEWS ITEM/PROGRAMME

Synopsis

Programme title ....
1. Programme code ....
2. Genre and country ....
3. Overall assessment of the portrayal of disability
   Negative   1   2   3   4   5   Positive
   0. Cannot code
   Include
   i) A brief explanation of the disabled character's role and relationship to the plot
   ii) The types of storyline involving the disabled characters, e.g. were the disabled characters involved in striving to achieve types of storylines or roles that necessitated them being cut off from society, etc.
   iii) Perceived metaphoric meanings connected with the portrayal
   iv) Basically was the portrayal positive, negative or neutral in terms of stereotypical imagery, sensationalism, exploitation, sentimentality, realism, depth to which the life of, and the difficulties faced by, the disabled person were shown, comparisons of the roles played by able-bodied and disabled characters, etc.
   v) Did there appear to be any particular reason for including the disabled characters?

Programme genre

Factual

1. News
2. Current affairs
3. Documentary
4. Magazine
5. Informational
6. Debate
7. Religious
8. Quiz
9. Art programme

10. Music/dance
11. Educational
12. Game show
13. Chat show
14. Sport
15. Special broadcast

Fictional

21. Crime/police/detective
22. Thriller
23. Spy
24. Western
25. War
26. Historical drama
27. Other drama
28. Sci fi
29. Horror
30. Soap
31. Avant-garde/art film
32. Comedy (stand up/sketches)
33. Situation comedy
34. Light entertainment
35. Cartoon
36. Children's drama
37. Children's other
38. Opera
39. Play
40. Fantasy
41. Real life cartoon

Appendix III
Group discussions and interviews with producers and writers

GROUP DISCUSSIONS

Group
A Youth workers – some with experience of working with people
  with disabilities, some without. White, black and Asian. Seven in
  group. Discussants from London and outside London.
B Young people – teenagers, 13–19. White, black and Asian.
  Twelve in group. London.
C Parents of children with disabilities. Bishop Stortford but
  including people from elsewhere, e.g. Cambridge. Nine in group.
D Centre for disabled. Mixed ages (young – early 20s – to elderly –
  60s). London. fifteen in group.
E Residential Centre for disabled. Young people – late teens and
  20s. Eight in group. Glasgow.
F Full-time workers with disabled people. five in group. Glasgow.
G Centre for disabled. Mixed ages – teens to 50s. Eighteen in group.
  Glasgow.
H Centre for disabled. Ages – 20s and 30s. Four in group. London.

In addition, more than a dozen people, most with disabilities, were
interviewed individually because of difficulties in creating groups for
discussion.

INTERVIEWS WITH PRODUCERS AND WRITERS

Discussions were held with five producers and three writers.
Correspondence took place with two producers and two writers. A
further eight letters requesting interviews with producers and writers
drew a blank.

Appendix IV
BBC survey questions

ASK ALL

Now some more general questions about people with disabilities.

29. When I say the word 'disabled', what do you think of?
     PROBE 'What else?' TWICE.

SHUFFLE SMALL PACK OF CARDS AND HAND TO INFORMANT

30. Here are some cards. Please sort them into two piles, those
     which you think are disabilities, and those which you think
     are not.

CODE BELOW, BUT ONLY ALLOW 'Don't know/it varies'
OPTION IF REALLY NECESSARY.

	Disability	Not a disability	Don't know/ it varies
Being in a wheelchair	1	2	3
Epilepsy	1	2	3
Severe short sight	1	2	3
Cerebral palsy (or spastic)	1	2	3
Missing or malformed limbs	1	2	3
Major visible scars	1	2	3
A bad back	1	2	3
Restricted growth (or dwarfism)	1	2	3
Total deafness	1	2	3
Partial deafness	1	2	3

Total blindness	1	2	3
Partial blindness	1	2	3
Mental handicap	1	2	3
Having difficulty walking or moving	1	2	3
Depression	1	2	3
Speech defects such as stuttering	1	2	3
Diabetes	1	2	3
Migraine headaches	1	2	3

SHUFFLE PACK AGAIN, THEN RETURN IT TO PLASTIC ENVELOPE
NON-TELEVISION VIEWERS GO TO Q. 33

31. SHOW CARD J

I am now going to read out a number of types of television programme. For each one, please tell me how often you think people with disabilities appear on them.

READ OUT IN TURN.

	Often	Occa-sionally	Hardly ever	Never	Don't know
Soap operas	1	2	3	4	5
Quiz shows	1	2	3	4	5
Documentaries	1	2	3	4	5
Sport	1	2	3	4	5
Situation comedies	1	2	3	4	5

TAKE BACK CARD J

SHOW CARD K

Now I'm going to read out a number of statements about people with disabilities. I would like you to tell me how much you agree or disagree with each one.

READ OUT IN TURN.

Agree a lot = 1
Agree a little = 2
Neither = 3
Disagree a little = 4
Disagree a lot = 5
Don't know = 6

(a) Large shops should provide
special facilities for disabled
people.   1   2   3   4   5   6

(b) Most disabled people
can live normal lives.   1   2   3   4   5   6

(c) Large companies should
always employ some people
with disabilities.   1   2   3   4   5   6

(d) People with disabilities
should appear on all types
of TV programmes.   1   2   3   4   5   6

(e) Most disabled people
need a great deal of help
in order to live normal lives. 1   2   3   4   5   6

(f) People with disabilities
should only appear on their
own, specialised TV programmes. 1   2   3   4   5   6

(g) There are too many drama
and soap programmes on
television which feature people
with disabilities.   1   2   3   4   5   6

(h) I sometimes get embarrassed
seeing severely disabled
people on television.   1   2   3   4   5   6

(i) There are too few drama
and soap programmes on
television which feature people
with disabilities.   1   2   3   4   5   6

(j) Certain types of disabilities
are too disturbing and should
not be shown on television.   1   2   3   4   5   6

TAKE BACK CARD K
ASK ALL

    33a.   Are you or is anyone else in your household a
             registered disabled, blind or deaf person?

Yes, informant	1
Yes, someone else	2
Yes, both informant and someone else	3
No	4

IF YES

    33b.   What is the disability?

    34a.   Do you or does anyone in your household have some
             permanent disability which limits them from getting
             about on their own and/or taking care of themselves?

Yes, informant	1
Yes, someone else	2
Yes, both informant and someone else	3
No	4

IF YES

    34b.   What is the disability?

    35a.   Do you know of anyone else such as a close relative or
             friend who is registered disabled or who has some
             permanent disability which limits them from getting about
             on their own and/or taking care of themselves?

Yes	1
No	2

IF YES

    35b.   What is the disability?

    36.   Do you look after disabled people as part of either
          voluntary or paid work?

Yes	1
No	2
Don't know	3

Notes

4 THE PORTRAYAL OF DISABILITY IN FICTIONAL PROGRAMMES

1 This episode is discussed further below, pp.127–128.

7 INTRODUCTION: DEFINITIONS AND STEREOTYPES

1 One ought to note that this statement is somewhat exaggerated. One discussant actually remarked how few disabled people one came across in the course of the day. A problem here is that some conditions which may be considered disabilities such as epilepsy and diabetes are not visible, while others such as paralysis or Down's Syndrome are clearly visible. This has obvious implications for television. How does one represent an epileptic or a diabetic without somehow making the 'disability' the central focus?

8 PUBLIC ATTITUDES TOWARDS THE PORTRAYAL OF DISABILITY ON TELEVISION

1 The A–E classification is a combination of occupation and employment status: A – profession; B – intermediate; C – skilled occupation; D – semi-skilled occupation; E – unskilled or unemployed.

10 A CLOSER LOOK AT RESPONSES TO THE PORTRAYAL OF DISABILITY ON TELEVISION

1 Personal communication by letter. The producer of *Coronation Street* and the producers of *Eastenders* refused to take part in this research.

References

BBC Broadcasting Research Department, *One in Four*, June 1987.

Bourdieu P., *Distinction*, Routledge & Kegan Paul, London, 1984.

Ellis J., *Visible Fictions*, Routledge & Kegan Paul, London, 1982.

von Feilitzen C., Strand H., Nowak K. & Andren G., 'To Be or Not to Be in the TV World: Ontological and Methodological Aspects of Content Analysis' in *The European Journal of Communication*, Vol. 4, pp. 11–32, 1989.

Greater Manchester Coalition of Disabled People (GMCDP), *Disabled People's Arts Conference*, Manchester, 1988.

Greenberg B.S., Simmons K.W., Hogan L. & Atkin C., *Life on Television: Content Analysis of US TV Drama*, Ablex, Norwood NJ, 1980.

Hartmann P. & Husband C., *The Mass Media and Social Attitudes*, ESRC report, Dec. 1972.

Head S.W., 'Content Analysis of Television Drama Programmes' in *The Quarterly of Film, Radio and Television*, Vol. 9, No. 2, pp. 175–194, 1954.

Longmore F., 'Screening Stereotypes: Images of Disabled People in TV and Motion Pictures' in Gartner A. & Joe T. (eds), *Images of the Disabled, Disabling Images*, Praeger, NY, 1987.

Martin J., Meltzer H. & Eliot D., *The Prevalence of Disability Among Adults*, Office of Population, Censuses and Surveys, HMSO, London, 1988.

O'Neill S., *Images of Disability*, Broadcasting Research Unit, unpublished, 1988.

Robinson J. & Levy M., *The Main Source. Learning from TV News*, Sage, 1986.

Scott-Parker S., *They aren't in the Brief*, King Edward's Hospital Fund for London, Kings Fund Centre, London, 1989.

Signorielli N., 'The Demography of the Television World' in Melischek G., Rosengren K.E. & Stappers J. (eds), *Cultural Indicators: An International Symposium*, Verlag der Österreichischen Akademie der Wissenschaften, Vienna, 1984.

Smythe D.W., 'Reality as Presented on Television' in *Public Opinion Quarterly*, Vol. 18, No. 2., pp. 143–156, 1954.

Sutherland A., *Disabled We Stand*, Souvenir Press, 1981.

World Health Organisation (WHO), *International Classification of Impairments, Disabilities and Handicaps*, 1980.

BROADCASTING RESEARCH UNIT PUBLICATIONS

Quality in Television – Programmes, Programme-makers, Systems
John Libbey/BRU (1989)

The Listener Speaks: The Radio Audience and the Future of Radio
by Steven Barnett and David Morrison
HMSO (1989)

Video World-Wide – an International Study
edited by Manuel Alvarado
UNESCO/John Libbey/BRU (1988)

Keeping Faith? Channel Four and its Audience
by David Docherty, David Morisson and Michael Tracey
John Libbey/BRU (1988)

Journalists at War: the Dynamics of News Reporting during the Falklands Conflict
by David Morrison and Howard Tumber
Sage (1988)

The Public Service Idea in British Broadcasting: Main Principles
BRU (1986)

School Television in Use
(forthcoming)

From Consensus to Competition: Readings in Public Service Broadcasting, 1923–87
by James McDonnell
Routledge (forthcoming)

BRU publications are now available from The Voice of the Listener, 101 King's Drive, Gravesend, Kent, DA12 5BQ

Index